POEMS for SHARING™

TEACHER NOTES

EARLY EMERGENT

19201 120th Avenue NE • Bothell, WA 98011

Poems for Sharing™ Teacher Notes: Early Emergent

We gratefully acknowledge Pam Bull for her contributions to these teacher notes.

Line illustrations by Cary Pillo

The Wright Group
19201 120th Avenue NE
Bothell, WA 98011

Printed in Canada

10 9 8 7 6 5 4 3 2 1

ISBN: 0-322-00512-4

Contents

Introduction to Poems for Sharing™

Poems for Sharing™ invites readers and listeners alike to enjoy the sound and meaning of words and to share this experience together. It is a collection of traditional and contemporary poems and songs for young readers. There are two sets—one for early emergent readers and one for upper emergent. Each set includes sixteen colorful posters and one teacher lesson plan booklet.

You will find a wide variety of poetry in Poems for Sharing, from nursery rhymes and contemporary poems by award-winning authors, to songs and traditional rhymes from other countries such as Malaysia and Japan.

This program is designed to enrich the classroom learning experience and provide additional literature for shared reading time. Numerous opportunities are provided to develop oral language, phonological awareness, letter-sound knowledge, and reading ability.

Phonological awareness is an important skill that involves hearing, distinguishing, and manipulating sounds in words. Many of the poems chosen for this collection have short, rhyming lines and a limited number of words to support students developing their phonological awareness and reading skills.

If you would like to find additional poetry for your classroom's poetry center, a list of titles is provided on page 70. Many of the books are anthologies that feature large selections of poems.

Wright Group books that are related thematically to the poems in the early emergent set are listed on pages 68–69.

What Do Children Learn from Poetry?

Poetry is a wonderful way to introduce children to the beauty of language. Like a book, a poem can tell a story and paint a picture in the mind. Poets play with words, sounds, meanings, and even the way words appear on the page, and all of these elements together make a poem a poem.

The best way for children to learn about poetry is to hear it, see it, say it, read it, and talk about it. Nursery rhymes, with their simple words and short rhyming lines, are a great beginning step for young readers. Children also love songs and poems that have strong rhythm, repetition, and memorable refrains. But children need to see and hear other poetic forms as well. Children can enjoy blank-verse poetry, which rhymes but doesn't have a regular rhythmic pattern, and free-verse poetry, which doesn't rhyme or have a regular rhythmic pattern or regular line lengths.

Who Was Mother Goose?

Several of the poems in the early emergent set for Poems for Sharing are nursery rhymes by Mother Goose, a famous poet whose existence has baffled scholars for years—many believe she was a fictional character. Some think she may have been a queen. Others believe that she was Elizabeth Goose, a woman who lived in colonial Boston in the late 1600s and loved to retell songs and rhymes from her childhood to her grandchildren. Regardless of the conflicting opinions, we do know that in 1781, John Newbery, an English publisher and bookseller for whom the Newbery Medal is named, printed a collection of rhymes titled *Mother Goose's Melody*. Since that time, the name *Mother Goose* has been firmly associated with nursery rhymes. We also know that many of the rhymes and verses originated in England and were based on folk songs, ballads, street cries, and pub songs.

Early Emergent Poems for Sharing Components

The early emergent Poems for Sharing components include the following items:

- **Sixteen poetry posters**
- **A five-day lesson plan for each poem**
- **A blackline master of each poem**
- **Sequencing and activity images**

Poems for Sharing Poetry Posters

Sixteen 17" x 22" posters are available at the early emergent level.

Poems for Sharing Lesson Plans

This booklet contains a five-day lesson plan for each of the sixteen poems in the early emergent set. The lessons will help students gain an understanding of poetic elements while learning skills in phonological awareness, concepts of print, phonics, word structure, vocabulary, and the mechanics of language. In addition, activities for creative writing, art, and movement are featured.

Biographical sketches of the poets and illustrators are also included for many of the poems. They are located at the end of the five-day lesson plans. You may choose to introduce this information on either Day Two or Day Three. And when available, additional verses or lines of the poems are also provided at the end of the lesson plans. These can be introduced to the students on Day Three or Day Four.

Blackline Masters of the Poems

A blackline master of each poem is provided. Students can color or illustrate the poem, practice reading it, and then take it home to read to a family member. If you wish, you can also make copies that the students can place in their own personal poetry books. At the end of the year the students will have a collection of their favorite poems.

The poem blackline masters can also be used at the listening center. Make a recording of a reading of the poem and place it in the listening center with copies of the poem. Invite students to play the tape and read along.

In addition to these ideas, students can also place copies of their favorite poems on a wall in the classroom that is designated for poetry. Encourage the children to read these poems during free reading or center time.

Sequencing and Activity Images

A blackline master page that features sequencing images or an activity is provided after the lesson plan for each poem. These images capture the most important features or events in each poem and can be used in any way that best meets the needs of your students. Suggestions for their use are written into the five-day lesson plans. For example, children can sequence the images in a pocket chart, attach them to ice-cream sticks and then match them to the words in the poems, or make stick puppets with them and dramatize the poems.

Overview of the Five-Day Lesson Plan

Day One

On the first day, you will introduce the poem. During this time, allow the students to savor the sounds, rhyme, and rhythm of the poem. You may choose not to show the poster of the poem to the students for this first reading so that the children focus on listening. You will also discuss the poem on Day One. Before you begin your discussions, you may need to read the poem a second time so that the children are more familiar with it. Discussion questions are provided.

Day Two

The second day includes a rereading of the poem, more discussion questions, a phonological awareness skills activity, and an integrated language arts activity. You can teach effectively through poetry as long as you keep the primary focus on the enjoyment of the poem. The integrated language arts activities such as writing innovations, drawing pictures and writing stories to go with them, exploring subject areas further with additional research, and creating murals allow children to respond to the poem through different modalities. If biographical sketches of the poets and illustrators are included at the end of the lesson plan, you may want to introduce this information on this day.

Day Three

On the third day the poem is reread. You may wish to introduce the sequencing images during the rereading. You will also continue to discuss the poetic elements of the poem and involve the children in a phonological awareness skills activity. A creative and fun integrated language arts activity is also provided on this day. If poet and illustrator biographical sketches are included at the end of the lesson plan, you may want to introduce this information to the students on this day. Additional verses or lines of the poems can also be read on this day.

Day Four

The poem is reread again on the fourth day, and children are encouraged to become involved with the reading. Activities such as choral reading and dramatization of the poem are suggested. You will also do two skills activities on Day Four. As on Day Two and Day Three, you will lead the children in a phonological awareness activity along with one other skills activity. Finally, you will conclude the poetry time for the day with an integrated language arts activity. If additional verses or lines to the poems are included at the end of the lesson plan, you may want to introduce them to the students on this day.

Day Five

On the last day, you will reread the poem again. You may choose to do the suggested rereading activity or have the children repeat one of their favorites from the week. One or two skills activities are included. On the fifth day you will also give each student a copy of the blackline master of the poem to color, illustrate, reread, and take home.

Little Boy Blue

Day 1

Introduce the Poem

Read the poem "Little Boy Blue" to the children. Try to reflect the natural rhythm of the poem as you read it through for the first time. Allow the students to absorb the language and think about what pictures the poem brings to mind. Discuss the illustration and any unfamiliar concepts or vocabulary such as *meadow* and the phrase "fast asleep."

Discuss the Poem

Invite the children to respond to the poem.

- **Can you describe a meadow?**
- **What is meant by "fast asleep"?**
- **Why do you think Little Boy Blue fell asleep?**
- **Do you like to take naps? If so, where?**

Day 2

Reread the Poem

Reread the poem "Little Boy Blue" with the children, encouraging them to join in when they feel comfortable. Continue to discuss the poem and the illustration.

Discuss the Poem

Encourage the children to think about the poem and the illustration.

- **Have you ever fallen asleep when you were supposed to be doing something else?**
- **What other animals live on a farm?**
- **What would happen if Little Boy Blue blew his horn?**

Focus on Phonological Awareness

Onset and Rime

Have the children locate Little Boy Blue in the illustration. Orally segment the onset */b/* from the sound that the rime *-oy* makes. Ask the children to do the same. Continue with one or two words that have the same rime, such as *Roy, soy, toy,* and *joy*. Have children brainstorm other words with the same rime.

Learn About Different Types of Horns

Bring in different types of horns to share with the children. If this is not possible, locate some photographs and information in books. Compare the different horns to the horn in the poster. Have each student draw a picture of his or her favorite horn and write about it.

Day 3

Reread the Poem

Read the poem and discuss the rhyming words. Point to the text to stress one-to-one correspondence and directionality. Invite the children to create hand motions for each line. Reread the poem with the hand motions. Allow individual children or groups of children to lead the rest of the students in additional rereadings using the hand motions.

Introduce the sequencing images on page 7 for "Little Boy Blue." Make photocopies and cut each image out. Write each line of the poem on a sentence strip and place the strips in a pocket chart. Have the children match the sequencing images to the respective words in the sentence strips.

Focus on Phonological Awareness

Rhyming

Read the poem out loud to the children, using the cloze technique to omit the words that rhyme with *horn (corn)* and *sheep (asleep)*. Say the lines of poetry up to the omitted words. Allow students to complete each rhyme with the missing word.

Brainstorm and Write

Have the children identify things in the poster that are blue (shirt, shorts, sky). Brainstorm other things that are blue and list them on a piece of butcher paper. Have children select an item from the list (or one of their own) to draw and then label with the following writing structure: A ____ is blue.

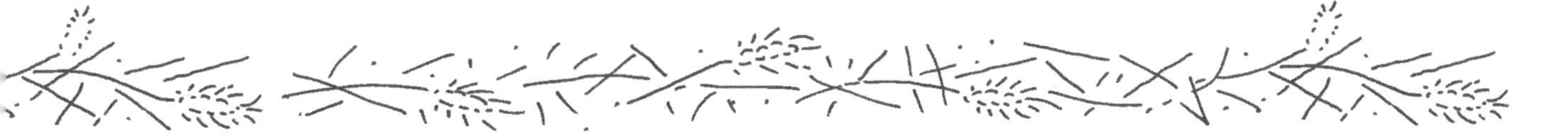

Day 4

Reread the Poem

Read the poem while pointing to the words. Invite the children to add sound or dialogue at the end of each line; for example,
Little Boy Blue, ("Where are you?")
Come blow your horn. ("Toot, toot!")
The sheep's in the meadow. ("Baa-baa!")
The cow's in the corn. ("Moo-moo!")
Where is the boy ("Yoo-hoo!")
Who looks after the sheep? ("Baa-baa!")
He's under a haystack, ("Ouch!")
Fast asleep. ("Zzzzz!")

Focus on Phonological Awareness

Phonemic Awareness: Initial Sound /k/

Invite the children to listen for words that begin with the /k/ sound as you reread the poem *(come, cow's, corn).* As children hear each word, have them pretend to blow a horn or snore.

Focus on Phonics

Initial Consonant c

Play "I spy" with the children. To begin, choose an object in the room that begins with the letter *c*. Say, "I spy with my little eye something that begins with *c*." The children take turns guessing. If an incorrect guess is given, say, "Yes, that begins with *c* but the thing I spy is_____." Give another clue such as "on the wall." The child who guesses correctly takes the next turn. Add the children's *c* words to a wall chart.

Make a Web

Little Boy Blue is responsible for looking after sheep. Discuss responsibilities that children have. List them on paper. Have each child make a web of his or her responsibilities. Children can illustrate and share their webs.

Day 5

Reread the Poem

Read the poem, pointing to the words as you read. Read each line first and then have children echo the line back to you. In rereadings, you can use different voices to read the poem. You may also wish to sing the poem. Music can be found in *The Reader's Digest Children's Songbook,* edited by William Simon, or *Complete Nursery Song Book,* edited by Inez Bertail.

Focus on Phonological Awareness

Phonemic Awareness: Segmenting and Blending

Play "What Am I Thinking Of?" Choose a word from the poem, orally segment the sounds, and ask the children to figure out the word. For example, you might choose the word *horn*. You would say, "I am thinking of a */h/ /or/ /n/*." The children must then blend the sounds together to form the word.

Focus on Vocabulary

Compound Word

Point to and discuss the compound word *haystack.* Have children frame the two words in *haystack* with a framing device. Then ask the children to find examples of other compound words. (You may wish to keep an ongoing list.)

Take a Poem Home

Give each child a copy of the poem on page 6 to color or illustrate, practice reading, and then take home to read to a family member. Copies of the students' illustrated poems can also be put into individual poetry scrapbooks that the children can make and decorate.

About the Poet

For more information about Mother Goose, see page 2.

About the Illustrator

As a child, Lauren Klementz-Harte loved doing pencil drawings of people. When she got older, she became an illustrator because she wanted to use her art skills in a practical way and to work with people, which she enjoys. She loves being part of something that will "help a child learn, perhaps, make that process more interesting or exciting, or maybe just make them smile." Her advice to children who want to be illustrators? "Work on your drawing skills...Build on your strengths, but...be willing to improve where you're weak. Don't be afraid to try something new..."

To create the illustration for "Little Boy Blue," Klementz-Harte used a *gouache (GWOSH)* and pencil technique. Gouache is a method of painting in which white is added to watercolor paint for an opaque effect.

Additional Lines

Will you wake him?
No, not I.
For if I do,
He's sure to cry.

Little Boy Blue

Little Boy Blue,
Come blow your horn.
The sheep's in the meadow.
The cow's in the corn.
Where is the boy
Who looks after the sheep?
He's under a haystack,
Fast asleep.

From the traditional rhyme

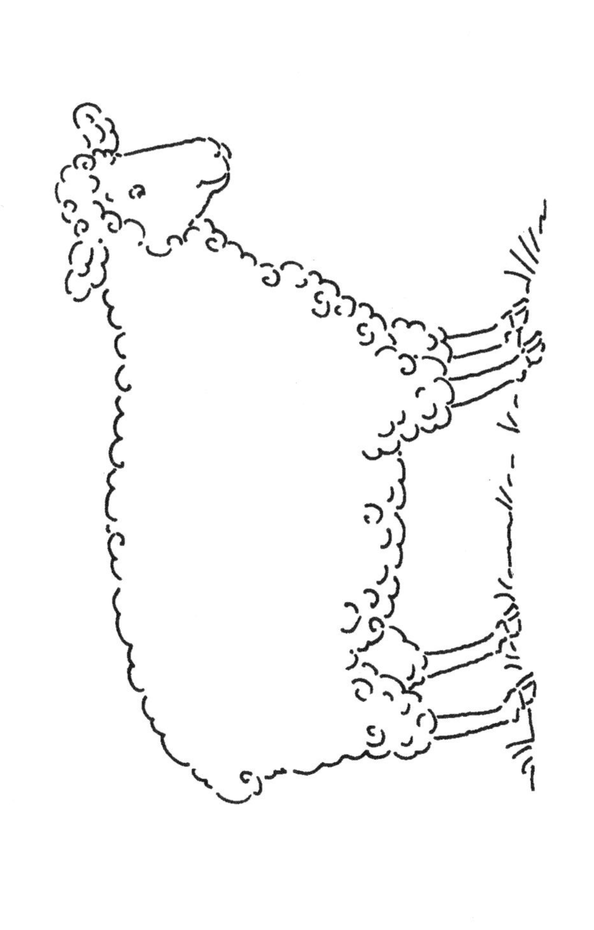

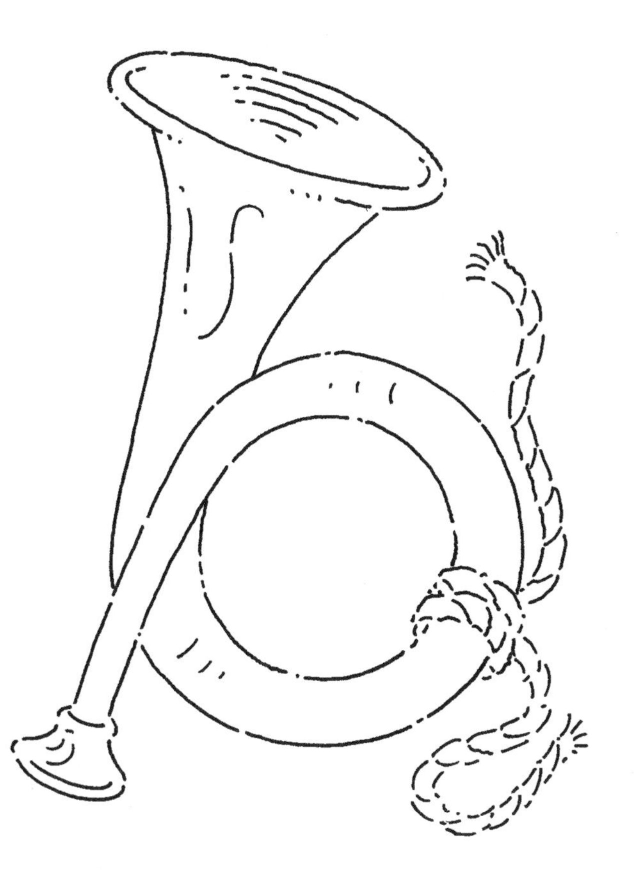

Just Like Me

Day 1

Introduce the Poem

Read the poem "Just Like Me" to the children. Try to reflect the natural rhythm of the poem as you read it through for the first time. Allow the students to absorb the language and to think about what pictures the poem brings to mind. Discuss the illustration and any unfamiliar concepts or vocabulary such as *pair.*

Discuss the Poem

Invite the children to respond to the poem.

- **How are the girls in the illustration alike and different?**
- **Do you see some things in the illustration that are pairs?**
- **How are you like these girls?**
- **What do you think is meant by "And there I saw a monkey"?**
- **What are some ways that you can "act like a monkey"?**

Day 2

Reread the Poem

Reread the poem "Just Like Me" with the children, encouraging them to join in when they feel comfortable. Call their attention to the repetitive line "Just like me" and discuss how repetition is used to show the two characters. Continue to discuss the poem and the illustration.

Discuss the Poem

Encourage the children to think about the poem and the illustration.

- **Would you agree that the girls in this poem are having fun? Why or why not?**
- **Can you think of a time when you acted silly like a monkey?**
- **Do you know someone who is a lot like you?**

Focus on Phonological Awareness

Rhyming

Read the phrase "pairs of stairs" from the third line of the poem. Have the children say the phrase, listening for the words that rhyme *(pairs, stairs).* Discuss how the words rhyme. Continue rereading the phrase, substituting words for *stairs* with words that rhyme and don't rhyme. Have the children listen to each phrase to decide if the words rhyme or not, such as "pairs of bears," "pairs of chairs," "pairs of monkeys," "pairs of hares," and "pairs of girls."

Draw a Picture and Write a Story

Have the children think about ways to act like monkeys. Brainstorm some of the silly things that the children have done in the past. Invite the children to draw pictures of themselves doing these silly things and then have them write about the pictures.

Day 3

Reread the Poem

Read the poem. Point to the text to stress one-to-one correspondence and directionality. Then read the poem again, inviting the children to say the refrain "Just like me" after you say the "I went..." lines.

Introduce the sequencing images on page 11. Make photocopies, cut the images apart, and attach them to ice-cream sticks. Invite the children to match the images to the corresponding words in the text as you reread the poem.

Focus on Phonological Awareness

Word Awareness

Read the poem to the children. Have them make a monkey face when they hear the word *me.*

Create a Poem Innovation

Invite the children to use the following poem structure to write their own poems: I went up/to/into the ________.

Day 4

Reread the Poem

Read the poem while pointing to the words. Then reread the poem and encourage the children to stand up and pretend they are doing the actions in the poem. Discuss the sequence of the poem.

- **What would happen to the poem if the lines were out of order?**
- **Why are the lines in this order?**

Finally, write each line of the poem on a sentence strip. Have children sequence the poem in a pocket chart.

Focus on Phonological Awareness

Phonemic Awareness: Initial Sound **/u/**

Say the first line of the poem and then repeat the word *up*. Ask children what sound they hear at the beginning of *up*. Then have the children sit in a circle. Fill a paper bag with items that have the */u/* sound and a few that do not. Pass the bag around the circle, stopping at each child. Have each child pull an item out of the bag, say what it is, and then decide if it has the short *u* sound.

Focus on Phonics

Initial Consonant **m**

Use the refrain "Just like me" to introduce the letter *m*. Have students find *m* in *me*. Then ask them to locate another word that begins with */m/*. Invite children to count all the *m* words in the poem.

Make a Book

Brainstorm things that come in pairs, such as shoes, socks, twins, feet, and hands. Write them on a piece of chart paper. Invite the children to select a word to illustrate. Then have each student complete the phrase "A pair of __________" with the word he or she illustrated and label the picture with the phrase. Allow the children to share and then bind the pages together to make a book.

Day 5

Reread the Poem

Read the poem while pointing to the words, this time allowing the children to be copycats. After you read each line, ask the children to repeat it. You can also select individual children to be the leader and have the rest of the class copy them. You might also choose to reread the poem again, this time skipping around the room with the children and stopping at the end of the poem to make monkey faces.

Focus on Phonics

Initial Consonant Blend **st**

Have students locate the *st* blend in *stairs*. Brainstorm other words that begin with the */st/* sound and add them to a word-wall chart.

Focus on Mechanics

Punctuation: Quotation Marks

Read the poem, line by line. Stop at the beginning and end of each line to discuss the quotation marks, which signify that someone is speaking. Then have the children identify who is speaking in each line. You may have to point out the use of red and blue text in the poem. Explain that the girl with the red shirt says the lines in red and the girl in the blue shirt says the blue lines.

Take a Poem Home

Give each child a copy of the poem on page 10 to color or illustrate, practice reading, and then take home to read to a family member. Copies of the students' illustrated poems can also be put into individual poetry scrapbooks that the children can make and decorate.

About the Poet

For more information about Mother Goose, see page 2.

About the Illustrator

Stacey Shuett was born on October 9, 1960. As a child, her family nurtured her artistic talents. She loved to do crafts and draw, and her father and grandfather taught her how to build things. For her eleventh birthday, her grandmother arranged for her to have oil painting lessons and she's been painting ever since! Being an illustrator for children allows Shuett to combine the two things she enjoys most—painting and using her imagination. Her advice to aspiring illustrators? "Do lots of drawing. The more you do, the better you'll get. Looking carefully at things will help your drawing skills, and drawing will help the way you see."

Shuett used acrylic paints on *gessoed (JE sohd)* paper to create the illustration for "Just Like Me." Gessoed paper is paper that has been prepared for painting by spreading a white paste mixture over it.

Just Like Me

"I went up one pair of stairs."
"Just like me."
"I went up two pairs of stairs."
"Just like me."
"I went into a room."
"Just like me."
"And there I saw a monkey."
"Just like me."

Traditional

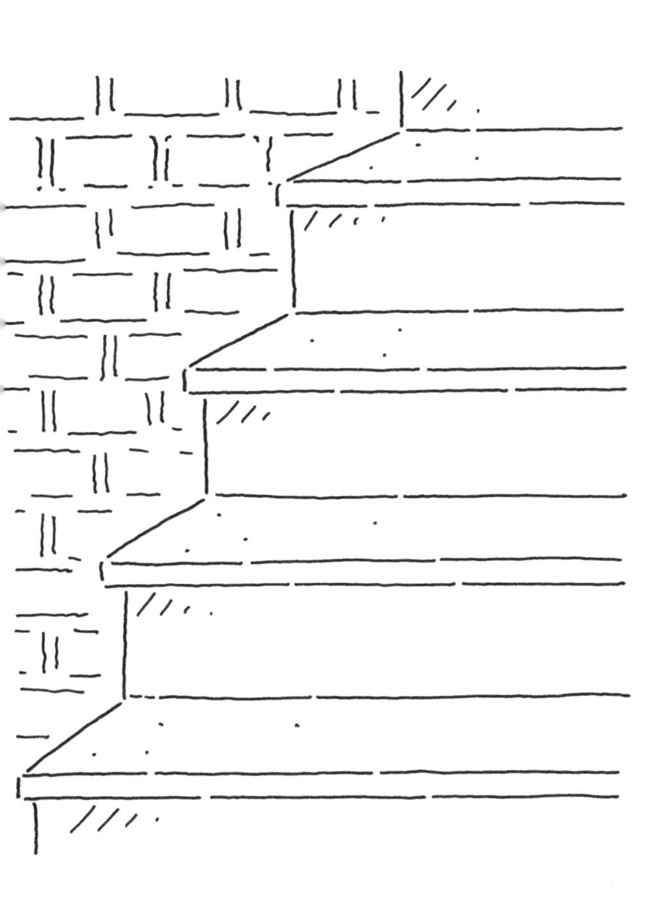

Blast Off!

Day 1

Introduce the Poem

Read the poem "Blast Off!" to the children. Try to reflect the natural rhythm of the poem as you read it through for the first time. Allow the students to absorb the language and to think about what pictures the poem brings to mind. Discuss the illustration and any unfamiliar concepts or vocabulary such as *launching mat.*

Discuss the Poem

Invite the children to respond to the poem.

- **What would you wear on a rocket ship?**
- **What does "Belts from head to toe" mean?**
- **How long do you think it would take to get to the moon in a rocket ship?**

Day 2

Reread the Poem

Reread the poem "Blast Off!" with the children, encouraging them to join in when they feel comfortable. Continue to discuss the poem and the illustration.

Discuss the Poem

Encourage the children to think about the poem and the illustration.

- **Have you ever seen a rocket blast off? Did it look like this?**
- **What do you think the person inside the rocket is feeling?**

Focus on Phonological Awareness

Rhyming

Use the cloze technique when appropriate so the children can hear the rhyming words *hat/mat* and *toe/go.* For example, read the line of the text up to the rhyme and stop. Allow the students to complete the line with the missing rhyming word.

Build a Rocket Ship

Have each child design a rocket ship or build a rocket ship in the block center and then write about the design.

Day 3

Reread the Poem

Read the poem. Point to the text to stress one-to-one correspondence and directionality. Read the poem again, this time encouraging the students to mime the poem or create hand motions for it. Then introduce the sequencing images on page 15 for "Blast Off!" Make photocopies, cut each image out, and attach them to ice-cream sticks. Have students match the images to the corresponding words in the poem as you reread it.

Focus on Phonological Awareness

Onset and Rime

Listen for the words in the poem that have the *-at* rime *(hat, mat).* Orally brainstorm additional words that rhyme with *hat* and *mat.*

Brainstorm Things for a Moon Trip

Brainstorm items you might take to the moon.

Day 4

Reread the Poem

Read the poem while pointing to the words. You may wish to have the children chorally read the poem, with one group reading the first four lines, another group reading the next four lines, and all of the children joining in on the countdown in the last three lines.

Focus on Phonological Awareness

***Phonemic Awareness: Initial Sound* /b/**

Invite the children to listen for words that begin with */b/* as you reread the poem. As they hear a */b/* word, have them jump up as if they are blasting off.

Focus on Phonics

***Initial Consonant* b**

Locate words in the poem that begin with *b*. Use a framing device, such as a fly swatter without the screen or a magnifying glass, to isolate the letter *b* each time it occurs.

Write a Story

Have each student write and illustrate a story about a trip to the moon in a rocket ship.

Day 5

Reread the Poem

Read the poem, pointing to the words as you read. You might want to encourage the children to take turns pointing to the words while you reread the poem.

Focus on Phonological Awareness

Syllable Awareness

Read the poem to the children. Have the children clap the syllables they hear as they read.

Focus on Vocabulary

Content Words

Write the numerals 1 to 10 on index cards or self-stick notes. As you reread the poem together, have students match the numerals to the number words in the poem.

Take a Poem Home

Give each child a copy of the poem on page 14 to color or illustrate, practice reading, and then take home to read to a family member. Copies of the students' illustrated poems can also be put into individual poetry scrapbooks that the children can make and decorate.

About the Poet

Cynthia Holley has had many occupations in her life. She has worked as a lifeguard, a newspaper columnist, a florist, a teacher, and a sales representative for The Wright Group. She is also a writer. "I like to write for children because children know how to have a fun time!" Holley was born on January 29, 1951. She lives in Matthews, North Carolina. When she was a child, she liked to write mystery and adventure stories. Reading other people's stories and wanting to see her own stories in a book inspired her to become a writer when she grew up. Her advice to young writers is simple. "Don't get discouraged. Most writers revise a story over and over and over and over!"

About the Illustrator

Because she was raised by two parents who were artists, it wasn't much of a surprise that Andrea Barrett would become an artist herself one day. As a child, Barrett drew pictures of family and friends. Today she lives in Kingston, Massachusetts, and she still continues to draw—for children. Her love of drawing fun objects and using bright colors led her to the occupation of illustrator. Barrett has some good advice for would-be illustrators. "Keep drawing and always let your imagination run free."

The illustration for "Blast Off!" was created using watercolor paints, *gouache (GWOSH)*, and colored pencil. Gouache is a method of painting in which white is added to watercolor paint for an opaque effect.

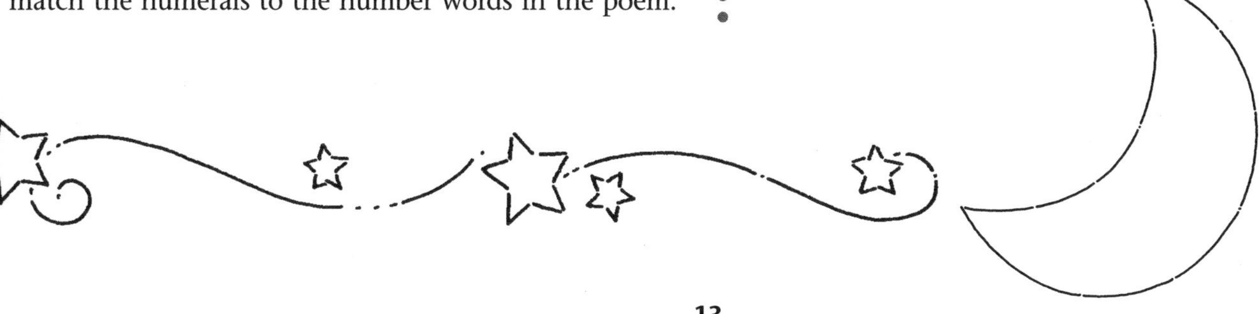

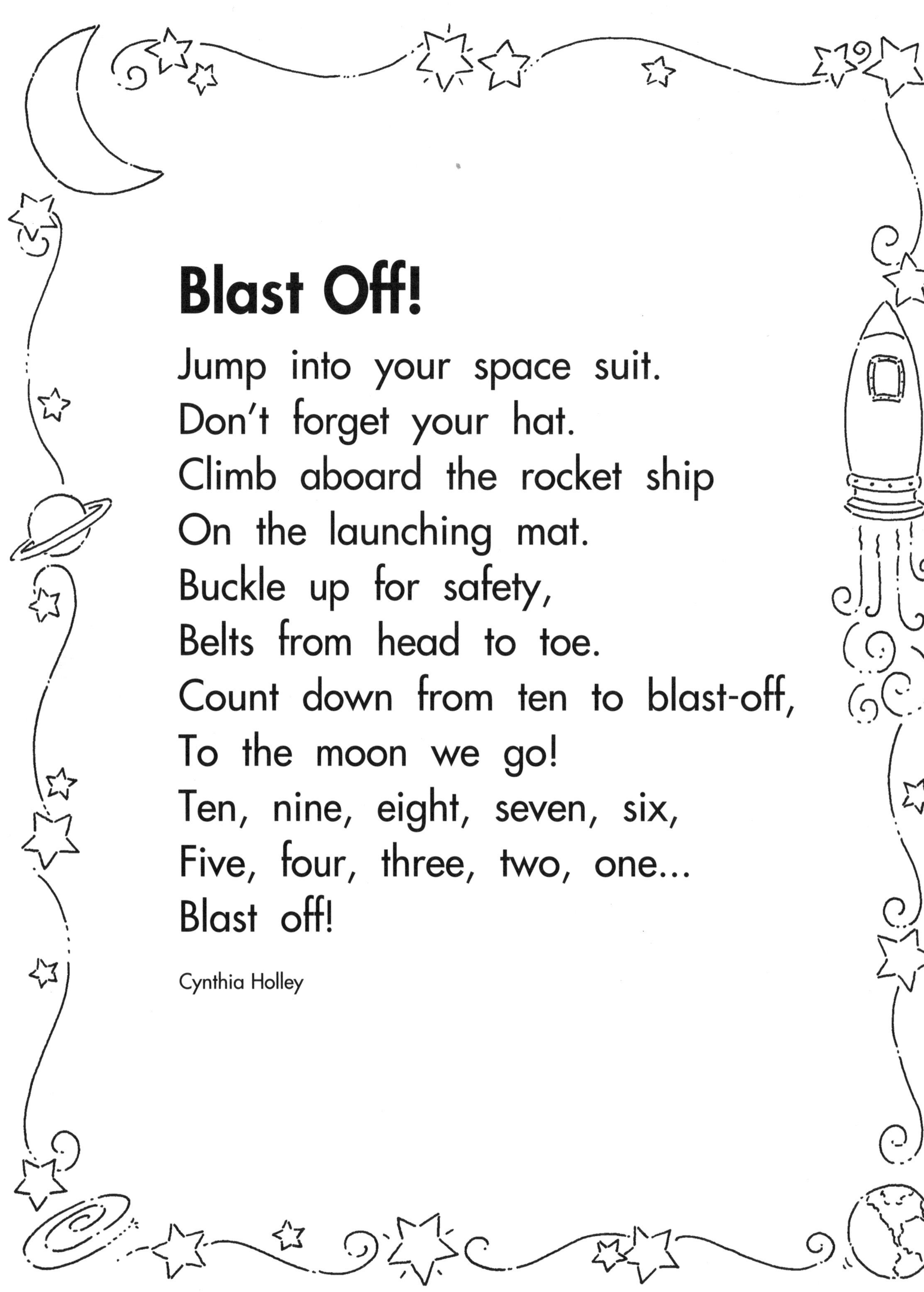

Blast Off!

Jump into your space suit.
Don't forget your hat.
Climb aboard the rocket ship
On the launching mat.
Buckle up for safety,
Belts from head to toe.
Count down from ten to blast-off,
To the moon we go!
Ten, nine, eight, seven, six,
Five, four, three, two, one...
Blast off!

Cynthia Holley

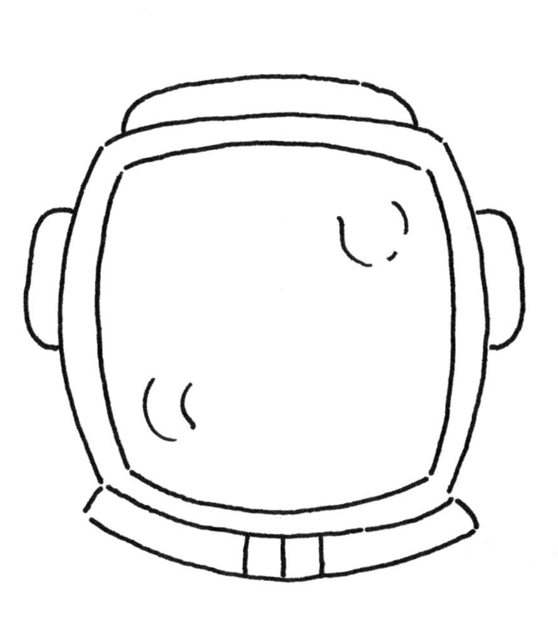

The Monsters' Garden Party

Day 1

Introduce the Poem

Read the poem "The Monsters' Garden Party" to the children. Try to reflect the natural rhythm of the poem as you read it through for the first time. Allow the students to absorb the language and to think about what pictures the poem brings to mind. Discuss the illustration and any unfamiliar concepts or vocabulary such as *garden rake.*

Discuss the Poem

Invite the children to respond to the poem.

- **What would you bring to the monsters' garden party?**
- **Do you think the monsters' garden party would be fun? Why or why not?**
- **What are some kinds of parties that you have been to?**
- **Can you think of things you would need for a party?**

Day 2

Reread the Poem

Reread the poem "The Monsters' Garden Party" with the children, encouraging them to join in when they feel comfortable. Continue to discuss the poem and the illustration.

Discuss the Poem

Encourage the children to think about the poem and the illustration.

- **How are the monsters in the poem alike and different?**
- **Which monster do you like the best? Why?**
- **Why did the monsters' garden party last so long?**

Focus on Phonological Awareness

Rhyming

Read the lines of the poem in pairs. Ask the children to listen for the rhyming words and tell you which ones they are.

Make Monster Masks

Have the children select their favorite monster from the poem and make a monster mask. You will have to cut out the eyes. Provide the children with many supplies to make and decorate the masks with, such as paper plates, ice-cream sticks to attach to the masks, construction paper, and paint. Invite the children to use their masks to dramatize the poem.

Day 3

Reread the Poem

Read the poem. Point to the text to stress one-to-one correspondence and directionality. Then introduce the sequencing images on page 19. Make a photocopy and cut out the images. You may want to enlarge the images on the photocopy machine. Attach the pictures to ice-cream sticks. Then select six children to be monsters and dramatize the poem with the pictures while the rest of the children reread the poem. Allow the children to take turns dramatizing the poem.

Focus on Phonological Awareness

Phonemic Awareness: Initial Sound /k/

Read lines two, four, and six of the poem. In each line, ask the children to listen for the word that begins with the /k/ sound (*cookies* in line two, *cake* in line four, *cupcakes* in line six). Then invite the children to think of additional words that have the /k/ sound.

Grow Monster Flowers

Have the children plant flower seeds in cups they have decorated to look like monsters. As the flowers grow, they will look like the monsters' hair.

Day 4

Reread the Poem

Read the poem while pointing to the words. Invite the children to clap to the rhythm of the poem. Then write each line of the poem on a sentence strip. Allow the children to sequence the poem in a pocket chart. You can also use the sequencing images on page 19 to sequence the poem or match them to the corresponding words in the poem.

Focus on Phonological Awareness

Line Awareness

Read the poem. Have the children listen for the end of each line. Give the children party favors similar to the ones in the illustration. When they hear the end of a line, encourage them to make noise with their party favors.

Focus on Phonics

Initial Consonant c

Have children frame the words in the story that begin with the *c* that makes a */k/* sound. If they frame the word *chocolate,* discuss the difference in the sounds. Then draw a large shape of a cake on butcher paper. Brainstorm words with the students that begin with *c* and write the words on the picture cake.

Write a Monster Riddle

Have the children work with a fellow classmate or an older student to write monster riddles. Point out that each of the monsters in the illustration is wearing a cap with a number on it. Have the pairs of students pick a monster in the poster and write clues in sentence form that describe their monster. Examples include the following sets of sentences:

I am purple.
I have spikes down my back.
I am carrying cupcakes.
Answer: I am Monster Six.

I am orange.
I have pointy ears.
I am carrying a tree.
Answer: I am Monster One.

Day 5

Reread the Poem

Read the poem, pointing to the words as you read. Then place blank self-stick notes over the number words in the monster names. Reread the poem and when you come to the blank notes, orally substitute the monster numbers with student names; for example, "Monster Amy brought the little green tree."

Focus on Phonological Awareness

Phonemic Awareness: Initial Sound /m/

Read the poem slowly. Have the children listen for words that begin with the */m/* sound. When the children hear a word with the */m/* sound, have them raise their arms like monsters and make monster sounds.

Focus on Vocabulary

Content Words

Write the numerals 1–6 and 10 on self-stick notes. As you reread the poem together, have the children match the numerals to the number words in the text.

Take a Poem Home

Give each child a copy of the poem on page 18 to color or illustrate, practice reading, and then take home to read to a family member. Copies of the students' illustrated poems can also be put into individual poetry scrapbooks that the children can make and decorate.

About the Poet

Marcie Bovetz makes her home in Woodinville, Washington. As a child, she loved to read all kinds of books—fiction, mysteries, fantasy, and biographies. She especially enjoyed the Little House books by Laura Ingalls Wilder. She also wrote a few stories and poems, and one summer created a neighborhood newspaper with a friend. Her interest in books and reading eventually led to her role as a writer.

Where do all her ideas come from? Well, Bovetz admits that coming up with initial writing ideas is hard for her. She tries to think of topics kids would be interested in and sometimes gets ideas from reading or events in the news. She has written many books for children and has found that there is one basic activity that anyone interested in writing must do—READ! Bovetz explains, "You can't become a writer if you aren't a reader first. Try to write and read every day. Make both part of your life."

About the Illustrator

Bob Byrd was born on January 11, 1942. He works out of his studio in Haddenfield, New Jersey. As a child he enjoyed creating very busy pictures—farms crowded with animals and circuses packed with performers.

Most of Byrd's ideas spring from his imagination. He enjoys illustrating for children because he's allowed to use his imagination to create little worlds, like the one for "The Monsters' Garden Party." Byrd created the illustration for this poster using pen and black ink with colored-ink washes. For those students interested in becoming illustrators, Byrd's advice is to "draw everything and read everything!"

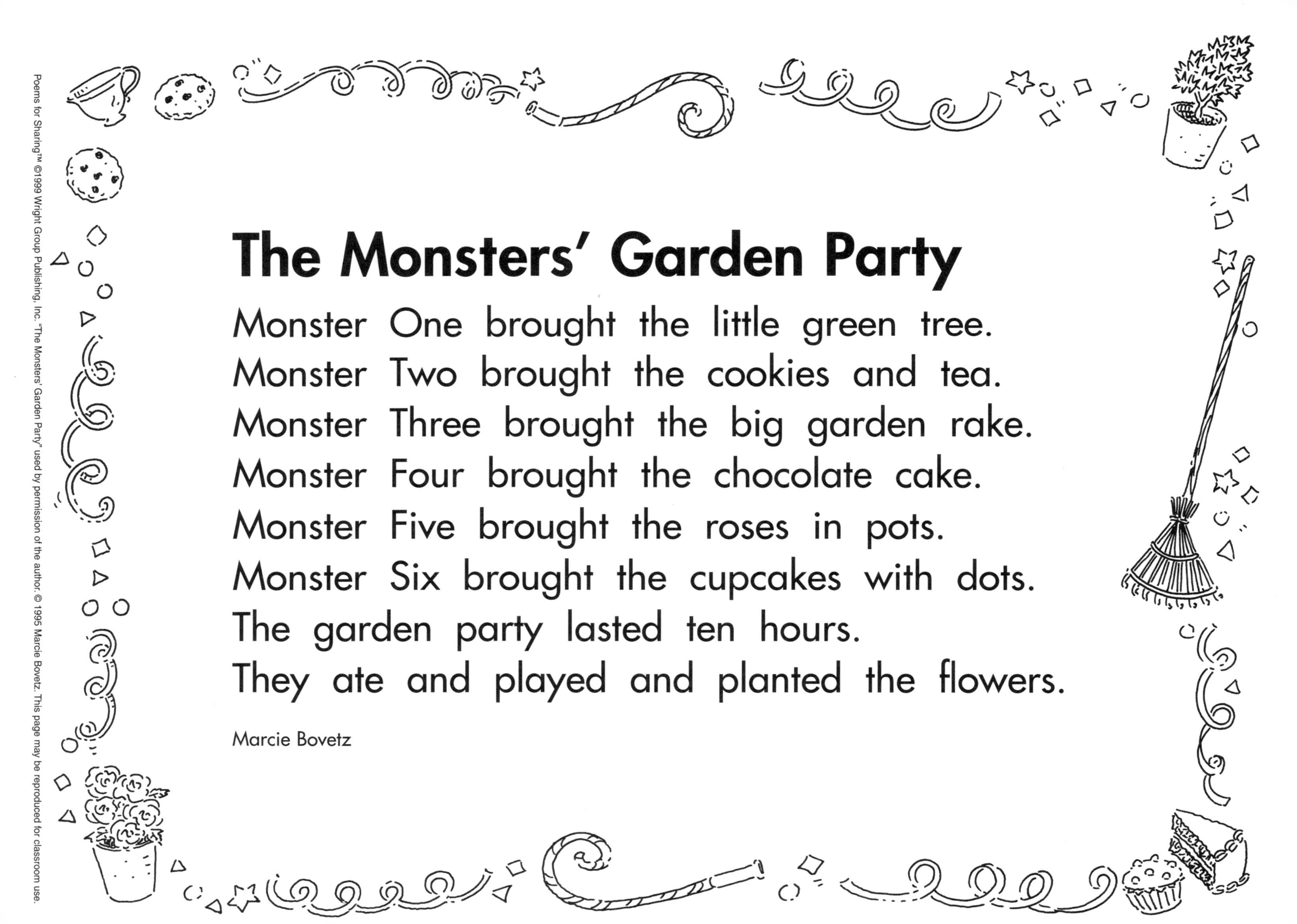

The Monsters' Garden Party

Monster One brought the little green tree.
Monster Two brought the cookies and tea.
Monster Three brought the big garden rake.
Monster Four brought the chocolate cake.
Monster Five brought the roses in pots.
Monster Six brought the cupcakes with dots.
The garden party lasted ten hours.
They ate and played and planted the flowers.

Marcie Bovetz

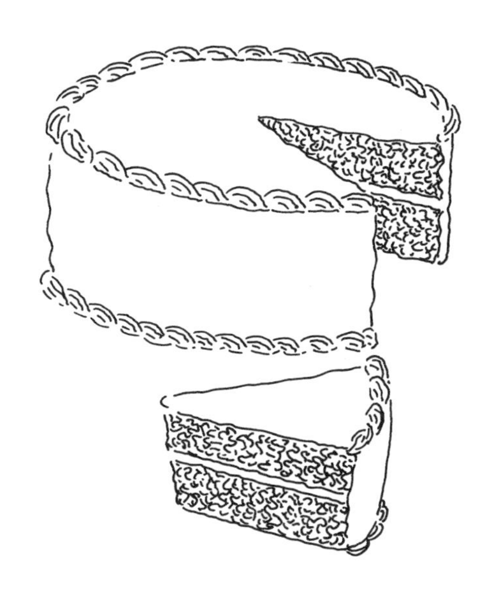

Mud

Day 1

Introduce the Poem

Read the poem "Mud" to the children. Try to reflect the natural rhythm of the poem as you read it through for the first time. Allow the students to absorb the language and to think about what pictures the poem brings to mind. Discuss the illustration and any unfamiliar concepts or vocabulary such as *squishy-squash* and *wade*.

Discuss the Poem

Invite the children to respond to the poem.

- **What does "All squishy-squash between the toes!" mean?**
- **Have you ever walked barefoot in the mud? How did it feel?**
- **Can you show me how you would *wade?***
- **Look at the illustration. What part of the rosebush is in the mud?**

Day 2

Reread the Poem

Reread the poem "Mud" with the children, encouraging them to join in when they feel comfortable. Continue to discuss the poem and the illustration.

Discuss the Poem

Encourage the children to think about the poem and the illustration.

- **Where does mud come from?**
- **How would you describe mud?**
- **Would you prefer to wade in mud or smell a yellow rose? Why?**

Focus on Phonological Awareness

Rhyming

Read the poem to the children. Have them listen for the words that rhyme *(toes, rose, knows)*. Encourage the children to orally compare and contrast the words. Ask them to describe how they are alike and different.

Make Mud Pictures

Provide the children with brown fingerpaint or chocolate pudding and white sheets of paper. Have the students create "mud" pictures. Encourage them to write about their pictures when they finish.

Day 3

Reread the Poem

Read the poem. Use a pointer that cleverly ties in with the poem, such as the tip of an umbrella or the stem of a plastic rose. Point to the text to stress one-to-one correspondence and directionality. Then read the poem again. This time encourage the children to create and then do hand motions for each line.

Focus on Phonological Awareness

Phonemic Awareness: Segmenting and Blending

Orally segment the word *mud*. Then have the children segment the word on their own. Ask them what sounds they hear at the beginning and end of *mud*. Finally, have the children blend the sounds together and say the word.

Create a Book About Mud

Children can't resist mud when they see it! Make some mud in a large bucket. Allow children to feel the mud. Then use a word web to record the children's responses as you brainstorm words that describe how mud feels. Have each child select one word from the word web to fill in the blank in the following sentence: "Mud feels _____." Invite the students to illustrate their sentences and bind them into a class book about mud.

Special note: If mud is too messy for you, consider doing the same activity with a yellow rose. Have the children describe how it smells, looks, or feels.

Day 4

Reread the Poem

Read the poem. Invite individual children to take turns pointing to the words while the rest of the children read the poem together. Encourage the children to read *squishy-squash* like the sound. Then read the poem again. This time have the children say *squishy-squash* at the end of every line.

Focus on Phonological Awareness

Phonemic Awareness: Initial Sound /m/

Have the children listen for words that begin with the /m/ sound. Encourage the students to wiggle their toes when they hear a word beginning with /m/.

Focus on Phonics

Consonant m

Use the blackline master of the poem to make a transparency copy. Place the poem on the overhead projector. Encourage the children to circle any *m* words they can locate in the poem.

Play Poetry Hopscotch

Have the children play hopscotch with the poem. Draw a large hopscotch outline on a sheet of butcher paper. Write one line of the text, in sequential order, in each box of the hopscotch outline. Have the children hopscotch through the poem, reading each line in the boxes.

Day 5

Reread the Poem

Read the poem, pointing to the words as you read. Encourage the children to clap, slap their knees, snap their fingers, or sway to the rhythm of the poem. Then write each line of the poem on a sentence strip and place the strips in a pocket chart. Introduce the sequencing images on page 23. Make three copies of the mud image, two copies of the toes image, and one copy of the rose image. Have the children match each image to the words in the text.

Focus on Phonological Awareness

Alliteration

Read line three of the poem to the children. Discuss the use of alliteration and ask them what words begin with the same sound. Brainstorm other things you can do in mud. Try to think of activities that begin with the same sound, such as "slide in slippery mud" or "bounce in beautiful mud."

Focus on Phonics

Initial Consonant w

Have children frame the two words in the poem that begin with *w (wade* and *wiggly).* Make a chart of additional words that begin with *w.* Then have students use these words to create alliterative phrases, such as "walk in wonderful mud" or "wash in warm mud."

Take a Poem Home

Give each child a copy of the poem on page 22 to color or illustrate, practice reading, and then take home to read to a family member. Copies of the students' illustrated poems can also be put into individual poetry scrapbooks that the children can make and decorate.

About the Illustrator

Obadinah Heavner works out of her studio in Seattle, Washington. As a child, she liked to play with clay and pipe cleaners. Apparently her fascination with clay hasn't diminished—she used plastalina, a modeling clay that never hardens, to create the illustration for "Mud." Ideas for Heavner's work come about by listening to music, drawing from the world around her, searching through many kinds of books, and brainstorming. She enjoys illustrating for children because of the "freedom, whimsy, and joy" she can put in the work. To the future artist, she shares this advice: "There are a lot of people with talent, but only those with some real *will* can find a place for themselves [as an illustrator]."

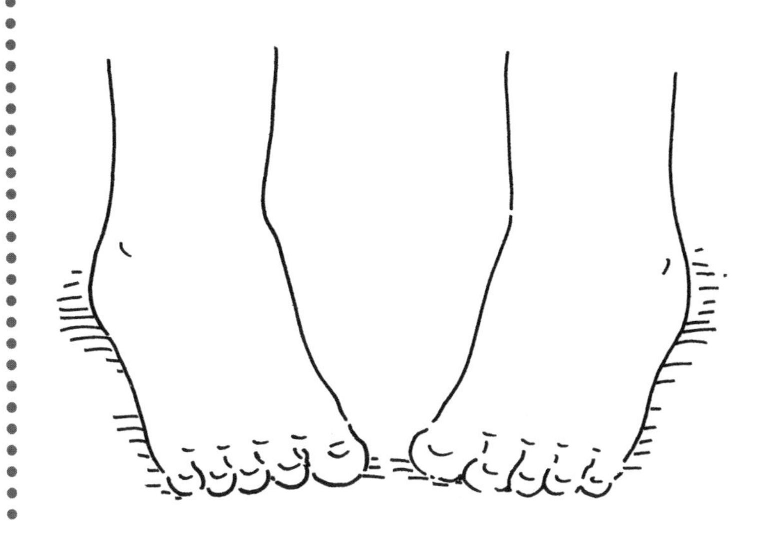

Mud

Mud is very nice to feel
All squishy-squash between the toes!
I'd rather wade in wiggly mud
Than smell a yellow rose.

Nobody else but the rosebush knows
How nice mud feels
Between the toes.

Polly Chase Boyden

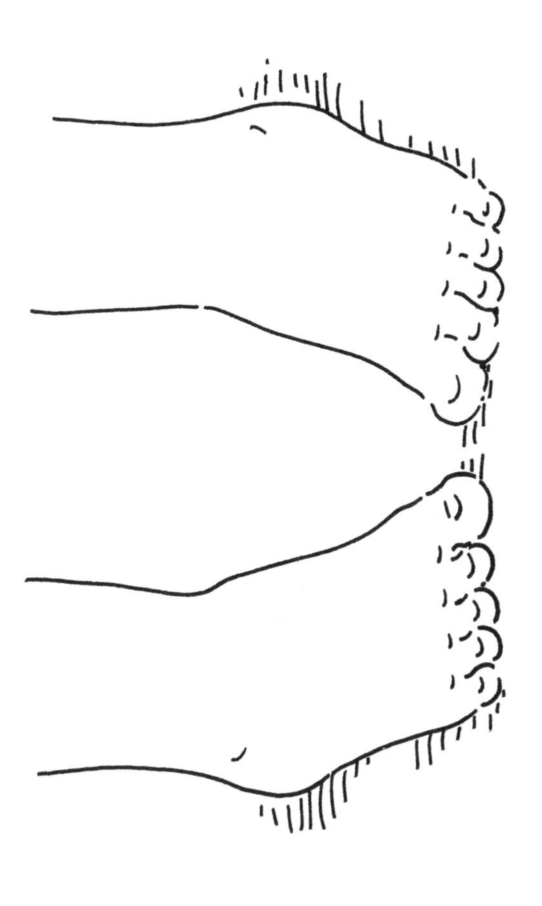

Covers

Day 1

Introduce the Poem

Read the poem "Covers" to the children. Try to reflect the natural rhythm of the poem as you read it through for the first time. Allow the students to absorb the language and to think about what pictures the poem brings to mind. Discuss the illustration and any unfamiliar concepts or vocabulary such as *covers* and *creep*.

Discuss the Poem

Invite the children to respond to the poem.

- **Can you show me what it means to creep?**
- **Why do you suppose blankets are also called covers?**
- **How do covers make you feel?**
- **Do you have a favorite blanket? If so, what makes it special?**

Day 2

Reread the Poem

Reread the poem "Covers" with the children, encouraging them to join in when they feel comfortable. Continue to discuss the poem and the illustration.

Discuss the Poem

Encourage the children to think about the strong images used in the poem and the illustration.

- **What is covering the cat?**
- **Can you think of other things that cover something else?**
- **What does "Nighttime covers all the things that creep" mean?**
- **Do you know of any animals that come out only at night?**

Focus on Phonological Awareness

Syllable Awareness

Read the poem. Have the children listen carefully and slap their knees, clap their hands, or tap their fingers in the air for each syllable they hear.

Write About a Favorite Blanket

Give each child a small square of plain white fabric. Invite the children to use fabric crayons to decorate the fabric to look like a favorite blanket. Then encourage the students to draw or paint pictures of themselves on paper and cut the pictures out. Attach each child's picture and fabric square to a piece of 8 1/2" x 11" paper, leaving space at the bottom for the child to write about his or her favorite blanket.

Day 3

Reread the Poem

Read the poem. Point to the text to stress one-to-one correspondence and directionality. Then encourage the children to think of hand motions to go with each line of the poem. Reread the poem, using the hand motions. Finally, invite small groups of children to perform the poem with the hand motions for the rest of the children.

Focus on Phonological Awareness

Phonemic Awareness: Segmenting and Blending

Slowly segment several words aloud from the poem such as *day, keep, make,* and *covers.* Have the children blend each word and tell you what the word is.

Bring and Show a Favorite Blanket or Stuffed Animal

Invite the children to bring and show to the class a blanket or a stuffed animal that they sleep with. Then have each child choose three words that describe his or her blanket or stuffed animal. Encourage the children to use these descriptive words to write poems about their blankets or stuffed animals.

_____(title)	My Blanket
_____(descriptive word)	Soft,
_____(descriptive word)	Warm,
_____(descriptive word)	Colorful,
__________(sentence)	I like my blanket!

Day 4

Reread the Poem

Read the poem while pointing to the words. Encourage students to play instruments such as a tambourine, drums, or bells to the rhythm of the poem. The poet Nikki Giovanni often uses jazz and blues rhythms in her poetry. If the children are not familiar with these forms of American music, you might want to play recordings by such famous jazz musicians as Louis Armstrong and Ella Fitzgerald. Encourage the children to compare the sounds and rhythms to the poem.

Write each line of the poem on sentence strips. Place the strips in a pocket chart. Then introduce the sequencing images on page 27, make photocopies, and cut them apart. Have the children match the images to the corresponding lines of text in the pocket chart. You may also want to encourage children to sequence the images and the sentence strips in the pocket chart.

Focus on Phonological Awareness

Rhyming

Use the cloze technique to have the children complete the rhymes in the poem *(away/day, creep/asleep).* Read the poem up to the beginning sound in *day* and then stop. Ask children to complete the rhyme. Then continue reading the poem up to the beginning sound in *asleep* and stop. Ask children to complete this rhyme.

Focus on Phonics

Word Family -eep

Have the children locate words in the poem that have the *-eep* rime *(keep, creep, asleep).* Then encourage students to use magnetic letters to make each word by changing the initial sound. Invite students to make other words with the same rime.

Brainstorm Places Where Animals Sleep

Discuss where the girl and the cat are sleeping. Talk about other places a cat might sleep. Brainstorm other animals and where they might sleep and write the responses on a piece of chart paper. Have each child select one animal from the chart. Ask the students to draw and then write about these animals.

Day 5

Reread the Poem

Read the poem, pointing to the words as you read. Have the children chorally read the poem. You might also want to invite the children to add sounds at the end of each second line, such as "brrr," "pitter patter," "creep," and "zzzzzz."

Focus on Phonological Awareness

Phonemic Awareness: Initial Sound /k/

Help students hear the initial consonant *c* sound */k/* in words from the poem.

- **What is the first sound that you hear in the word *covers?***

Then read the poem. As students hear a word with the */k/* sound, ask them to pretend to cover themselves up or cover a part of their body (nose, mouth) with their hands.

Focus on Phonics

Initial Consonant c

Have the children brainstorm words that begin with the */k/* sound. Encourage the children to create a list with these words and words from the poem. Then have each student pick a word from the list, write it on a blank piece of paper, and illustrate it. Bind the drawings together to make a word book.

Take a Poem Home

Give each child a copy of the poem on page 26 to color or illustrate, practice reading, and then take home to read to a family member. Copies of the students' illustrated poems can also be put into individual poetry scrapbooks that the children can make and decorate.

About the Poet

Nikki Giovanni was born in Knoxville, Tennessee, on June 7, 1943. She is a poet, essayist, and children's writer and has devoted much of her writing to the experiences of African Americans living in American cities. Listen carefully to the rhythm of "Covers," and you just might hear a little taste of jazz and blues that is often present in Giovanni's poetry.

About the Illustrator

Siri Weber Feeney was born on March 24, 1956. From an early age she was encouraged to write and illustrate her own books. By the time she was six, Feeney knew she wanted to create children's books someday.

To create the illustration for "Covers," Feeney used colored pencils, crayons, and oil pastels on darkly tinted *gessoed (JE sohd)* paper. Gessoed paper is paper that has been prepared by painting a paste mixture over it.

For children interested in pursuing a career in illustration, she advises them to practice. "The more practice you have, the better you'll do. And the better you do, the more fun you'll have doing it! It's very much like a sport, really; your hands and eyes need practice 'talking' to each other."

Covers

Glass covers windows
to keep the cold away
Clouds cover the sky
to make a rainy day

Nighttime covers
all the things that creep
Blankets cover me
when I'm asleep

Nikki Giovanni

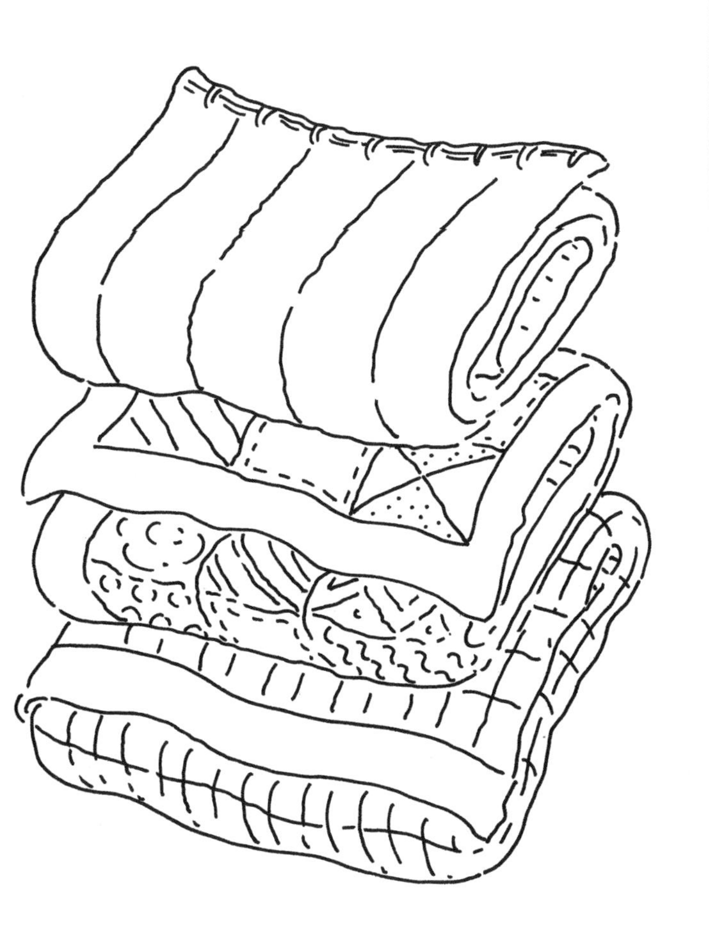

The Bus Song

Day 1

Introduce the Poem

Read the poem "The Bus Song" to the children. Try to reflect the natural rhythm of the poem as you read it through for the first time. Allow the students to absorb the language and to think about what pictures the poem brings to mind. Discuss the illustration and any unfamiliar concepts or vocabulary such as *'round.*

Discuss the Poem

Invite the children to respond to the poem.

- **Have you ever taken a ride on a bus like this before? If so, where were you going?**
- **Can you think of some places where the bus in this illustration might stop?**
- **Who do you think might be riding the bus?**

Day 2

Reread the Poem

Reread the poem "The Bus Song" with the children, encouraging them to join in when they feel comfortable. Continue to discuss the poem and the illustration.

Discuss the Poem

Encourage the children to think about the poem and the illustration.

- **Do you like riding on a bus? Why or why not?**
- **Why do people ride buses?**

Focus on Phonological Awareness

Phonemic Awareness: Segmenting and Blending

Ask the children, "What word from the poem would you have if we put these sounds together: */b/ /u/ /s/?"* Continue in the same manner with other words from the poem *(song, wheels, 'round,* and *town).*

Make a Book

Invite the children to brainstorm things that are round. List them on a piece of chart paper. Then have each child draw a picture of one thing from the list and write a sentence about it; for example, "A _____ is round." Let the students share their sentences and then bind them together to make a book titled "Things That Are Round."

Day 3

Reread the Poem

Sing the poem. Point to the words to stress one-to-one correspondence and directionality. Encourage the children to think of hand motions to go with the poem. Then sing the poem again, this time including the hand motions. Introduce the sequencing images on page 31 for the poem. Make photocopies and cut them apart. Attach the images to ice-cream sticks. Invite the children to match the images to the corresponding words in the text as you sing the song.

Focus on Phonological Awareness

Initial Sound /r/

Ask students to listen as you read the poem.

- **What word is repeated several times?**
- **What sound do you hear at the beginning of *'round?***
- **What other words do you know that begin with */r/?***

Create a Poster

Brainstorm bus safety rules with the children and list them on a piece of butcher paper. Have each child select one safety rule and design and create a poster for it.

Day 4

Reread the Poem

Sing "The Bus Song" again, pointing to the words. Provide instruments such as drums, tambourines, bells, and maracas that the children can play to the rhythm of the poem.

Focus on Phonological Awareness

Word Awareness

Read the poem aloud to the children. Have them clap once for each word they hear.

Focus on Concepts of Print

Concept of Word

Discuss how words are often repeated in a poem to make it more fun to read. Have the children find the word *'round* and count the number of times the word appears in the poem.

Write an Innovation

Help the children write an innovation of "The Bus Song." Use the following structure from the poem:

The _____ on/in the _____ go/goes _____ and _____,
_____ and _____, _____ and _____.
The _____ on/in the _____ go/goes _____ and ____, All through the town.

Day 5

Reread the Poem

Sing the poem, holding hands and walking in a circle. Next, sing the poem again, this time going the other direction. Have the children sit down. Write additional verses to the poem on chart paper. Then read the additional verses to the poem while pointing to each verse. Invite the children to create hand motions for the new verses and then sing the new verses while doing the hand motions.

Focus on Mechanics

Capitalization

Write each line of the poem on sentence strips. Then write the word *'round* on seven blank strips of paper and write the word *'Round* with a capital *R* on one strip. Place the lines of the poem in a pocket chart. Have the children distinguish between the uppercase *R* and lowercase *r* by matching the individual words to the words in the lines of the poem.

Take a Poem Home

Give each child a copy of the poem on page 30 to color or illustrate, practice reading, and then take home to read to a family member. Copies of the students' illustrated poems can also be put into individual poetry scrapbooks that the children can make and decorate.

About the Illustrator

Tim Egan was born on September 24, 1957. As a child, he liked to draw animals. When he grew up, he was encouraged by his father to pursue a career in art. Egan works out of his home studio in Canoga Park, California, surrounded by his dog, cats, chickens, and fish. He loves illustrating for children. It gives him a great sense of freedom to turn his ideas into books and posters. However, Egan's ideas for projects often appear at strange times, like when he's driving or just about to fall asleep. If he weren't an illustrator, Egan says he would still like to be involved in creating books but probably as the author. The illustration for "The Bus Song" was created using india ink and watercolor paints. His advice to children interested in becoming illustrators is honest. "Keep drawing and realize that mistakes are part of the process. I still make them every day."

Additional Verses

The people on the bus go up and down...
The horn on the bus goes toot-toot-toot...
The money in the box goes ding-ding-ding...
The wipers on the bus go swish-swish-swish...
The driver on the bus says, "Move on back..."

The Bus Song

The wheels on the bus go 'round and 'round,
'Round and 'round, 'round and 'round.
The wheels on the bus go 'round and 'round
All through the town.

From the traditional song

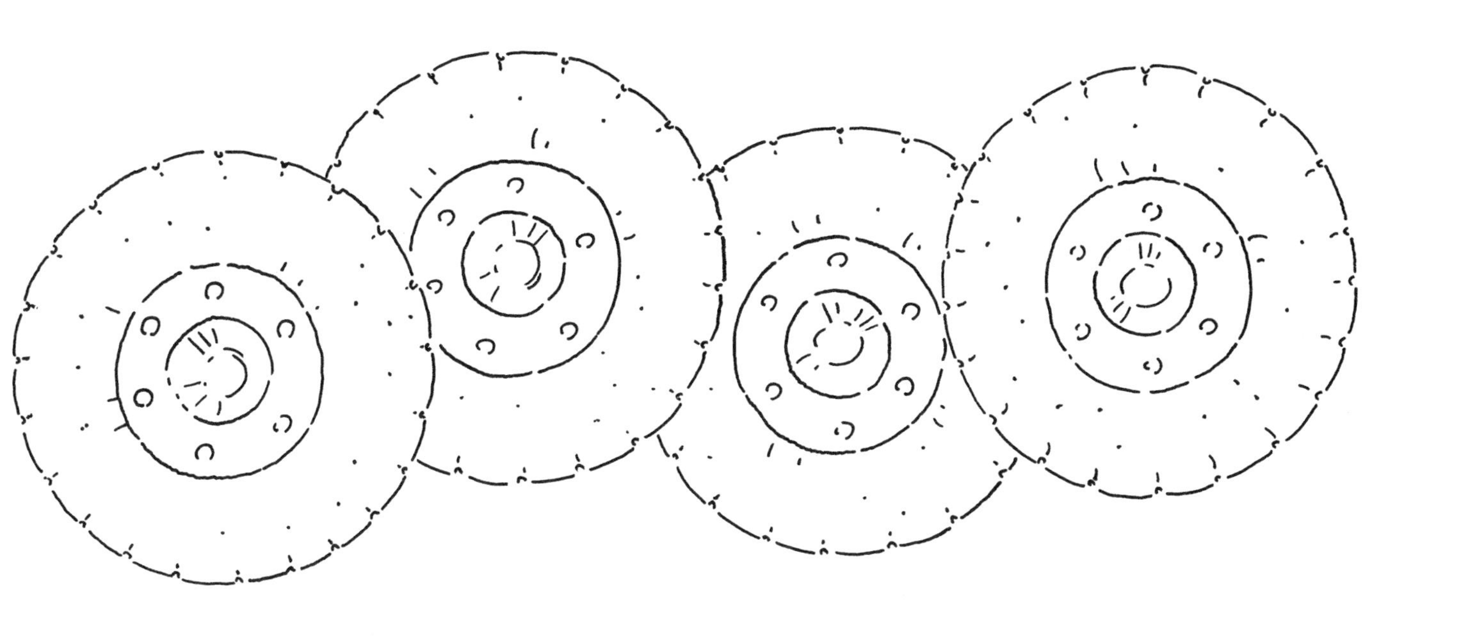

Fiddle-i-fee

Day 1

Introduce the Poem

Read the poem "Fiddle-i-fee" to the children. Try to reflect the natural rhythm of the poem as you read it through for the first time. Allow the students to absorb the language and to think about what pictures the poem brings to mind. Discuss the illustration and any unfamiliar concepts or vocabulary such as *pleased* and *yonder*.

Discuss the Poem

Invite the children to respond to the poem.

- **What does "yonder tree" mean?**
- **How do you think the animals pleased the boy?**
- **What is the boy feeding his pets?**
- **Do you have a pet? If so, what do you feed it?**

Day 2

Reread the Poem

Reread the poem "Fiddle-i-fee" with the children, encouraging them to join in when they feel comfortable. Continue to discuss the poem and the illustration.

Discuss the Poem

Encourage the children to think about the poem and the illustration.

- **Have you ever heard a cat go "fiddle-i-fee"?**
- **Have you ever heard a hen go "chimmy-chuck"?**
- **Have you ever heard a duck go "quack, quack"?**
- **What sounds do these animals make?**

Focus on Phonological Awareness

Phonemic Awareness: Compare/Contrast

Have the children listen to the words *my* and *by* from the poem to determine if they end with the same sound. Say each word separately, slowly articulating each sound: /m/ /ī/, /b/ /ī/. Ask the children what they hear.

- **Do *my* and *by* end with the same sound? What sound is it?**

Write a Poem

Invite the children to brainstorm animals and the sounds that they make. List them on a piece of butcher paper. Then write the following structure to the poem on large sheets of butcher paper:

I had a _____ and the _____ pleased me. I fed my _____ by yonder tree. _____ goes _____, _____.

Encourage the children to help you fill in the blank spaces using the words from the brainstorming list. Then ask the children to illustrate their poems.

Day 3

Reread the Poem

Read the poem together, pointing to the text to stress one-to-one correspondence and directionality. You may also wish to sing the poem. Music can be found in the *Complete Nursery Song Book,* edited by Inez Bertail.

Focus on Phonological Awareness

Rhyming

Read the poem to the children. Have them listen for the words that rhyme *(me, tree, fee).* Encourage children to think of other words that rhyme.

Write About Favorite Foods

Have the children search through magazines to find and cut out pictures of things they like to eat. Then give each child a piece of paper with the sentence, "I like to eat _________." Encourage the children to glue their pictures onto the paper and fill in the blank. Children can also draw a picture of themselves next to their favorite foods.

Day 4

Reread the Poem

Read the poem while pointing to the words. Discuss how alliteration is used throughout the poem. Then introduce the sequencing images on page 35. Make photocopies of them, cut them apart, and attach each image to a headband made out of a strip of construction paper. Invite students to take turns wearing the headbands and dramatizing the poem as the other children reread it.

Focus on Phonological Awareness

Phonemic Awareness: Manipulating

Select a consonant sound to replace the */f/* sound in *fiddle-i-fee.* Read the poem to the children, substituting the sound to make another nonsense word, such as */t/* for *tiddle-i-tee.* Invite the children to suggest more sounds. Reread the poem each time.

Focus on Concepts of Print

Capitalization

Point out the capital letters in the poem, one at a time: *I, C, H, D.* Have students locate the matching lowercase letter in the text with a framing device such as their fingers or a fly swatter without a screen.

Make a Picture Graph

Have each child draw a picture of his or her favorite farm animal. Use the pictures to make a picture graph titled "Our Favorite Farm Animals."

Day 5

Reread the Poem

Point to the words as you read the poem. Discuss the repetition of the last line in each verse and how it is used. Encourage the children to sway, rock side to side, or rock back and forth to the rhythm. Then make a photocopy of the sequencing images on page 35 and cut them apart. Attach them to ice-cream sticks. Have the children match each image to the corresponding word in the text as you reread the poem.

Focus on Phonological Awareness

Phonemic Awareness: Blending

Select an animal from the poem. Say, "I am thinking of an animal from the poem. It is a */k/ /a/ /t/.*" (Slowly articulate each sound.) Encourage the children to blend the sounds together to figure out the word. Continue with the other two animal words from the poem. Then invite the children to continue, using other farm animal names.

Focus on Phonics

Word Family -uck

Point out the words *duck* and *chuck* in the poem. Discuss that they have the same word family but different beginning sounds. Have the children identify the word family *-uck.* Have the children brainstorm as many *-uck* word-family words as they can. List the words on a wall chart. Encourage students to also search through books and magazines to find other words from the same word family. Add them to the list.

Take a Poem Home

Give each child a copy of the poem on page 34 to color or illustrate, practice reading, and then take home to read to a family member. Copies of the students' illustrated poems can also be put into individual poetry scrapbooks that the children can make and decorate.

About the Poet

For more information about Mother Goose, see page 2.

About the Illustrator

G. Brian Karas was born on September 27, 1957. Karas works out of his home studio in Rhinebeck, New York. When he was a child, Karas loved to draw the characters from the comic strip Peanuts. Now he is illustrating for children and hopes that his illustrations influence children in a positive way. He is encouraging to those interested in becoming illustrators. "Follow your instincts. If you want to be an illustrator, go after it."

Karas chose to create the illustration for "Fiddle-i-fee" using acrylic paints, pencil, and a technique called *gouache (GWOSH).* Gouache is a method of painting in which white is added to watercolor paint for an opaque effect.

Additional Verse

I had a goose and the goose pleased me.
I fed my goose by yonder tree.
Goose goes swishy, swashy.
Duck goes quack, quack.
Hen goes chimmy-chuck, chimmy-chuck.
Cat goes fiddle-i-fee.

Fiddle-i-fee

I had a cat and the cat pleased me.
I fed my cat by yonder tree.
Cat goes fiddle-i-fee.

I had a hen and the hen pleased me.
I fed my hen by yonder tree.
Hen goes chimmy-chuck, chimmy-chuck.
Cat goes fiddle-i-fee.

I had a duck and the duck pleased me.
I fed my duck by yonder tree.
Duck goes quack, quack.
Hen goes chimmy-chuck, chimmy-chuck.
Cat goes fiddle-i-fee.

From the traditional rhyme

Milk

Hey, Diddle, Diddle!

Day 1

Introduce the Poem

Read the poem "Hey, Diddle, Diddle!" to the children. Try to reflect the natural rhythm of the poem as you read it through for the first time. Allow the students to absorb the language and to think about what pictures the poem brings to mind. Discuss the illustration and any unfamiliar concepts or vocabulary such as *sport* and *fiddle* and the nonsense word *diddle.*

Discuss the Poem

Invite the children to respond to the poem.

- **What do you think "to see such sport" means?**
- **Which things in the illustration could really happen? Which are make-believe? How do you know?**

Day 2

Reread the Poem

Reread the poem "Hey, Diddle, Diddle!" with the children, encouraging them to join in when they feel comfortable. Continue to discuss the poem and the illustration.

Discuss the Poem

Encourage the children to think about the poem and the illustration. Discuss how personification is used to bring the animals to life.

- **Have you ever seen or heard a fiddle before? If so, where?**
- **What are some things that make you laugh?**
- **What would you do if you saw a cat playing a fiddle, a cow jumping over the moon, or a dish running away with a spoon?**

Focus on Phonological Awareness

Word Awareness

Read the poem slowly to the children. Have the children pretend to play a fiddle, moving the bow back and forth once for each word that they hear.

Brainstorm Make-Believe Animal Actions

Discuss the make-believe things that the animals in this poem do. Invite the children to brainstorm additional animals and silly make-believe things they could do. Have each child select one animal to draw. Then invite the students to write something about their animals.

Day 3

Reread the Poem

Read the poem. Point to the text to stress one-to-one correspondence and directionality. Encourage the children to create hand motions for each line. Reread the poem using the hand motions. Then introduce the sequencing images on page 39, make photocopies, and cut them apart. Write each line of the poem on a sentence strip and then place the strips in a pocket chart. Have the children match the sequencing images to the corresponding lines of text in the pocket chart. Children can also sequence both the images and the text.

Focus on Phonological Awareness

Phonemic Awareness: Initial Sounds /sp/

Say the words *sport* and *spoon* from the poem. Then ask the children what sounds they hear at the beginning of the words. Encourage children to think of additional words that begin with the */sp/* sound.

Learn About the Fiddle

Share a real fiddle with the children if one is available, or a picture of one. Invite someone to come in and play a fiddle, or play a recording of fiddle music. Invite the children to write about the experience and draw a picture to go with their writing.

Day 4

Reread the Poem

Read the poem while pointing to the words. Encourage children to sing the poem. If you don't know the tune, you can find the music in *The Reader's Digest Children's Songbook,* edited by William Simon, or *Complete Nursery Rhyme Song Book,* edited by Inez Bertail.

Make another set of sequencing images found on page 39 and cut them apart. Attach them to ice-cream sticks and invite the children to use the images to recite the poem.

Focus on Phonological Awareness

Phonemic Awareness: Medial Sound /i/

Say words from the poem that contain the short *i* sound, as well as several others that do not, such as *diddle, fiddle, little, dish, cat,* and *dog.* Slowly articulate each word. Ask the children to pretend to play a fiddle when they hear a word with the /i/ sound in it.

Focus on Vocabulary

Content Words

Have the children match pictures to words from the poem. Make photocopies of the blackline master of the poem on page 38 and give each child a copy. Encourage the children to draw a line from each picture to its corresponding word in the text.

Day 5

Reread the Poem

Read the poem, pointing to the words as you read. Then invite individual children to pantomime lines of the rhyme as the other children try to guess which line they are performing.

Make a Mural

Invite the children to make a mural of the poem. Use large sheets of butcher paper for the background. Encourage the children to paint or draw each character from the poem and place the characters on the mural background. Add speech bubbles to each character and have the children brainstorm things that the characters might say, such as "Where should we go?" for the dish and the spoon.

Focus on Phonological Awareness

Rhyming

Have the children listen for words that rhyme as you read the poem *(diddle/fiddle, moon/spoon).* Invite children to brainstorm additional words that rhyme with each pair.

Focus on Vocabulary

Multiple Meaning Word

Discuss the multiple meanings of the word *sport* (to amuse oneself; a physical activity such as baseball or soccer; someone who takes news well). Give examples of each definition, including the way the word is used in "Hey, Diddle, Diddle!" Ask the children to think of other examples. Then encourage each student to draw a picture that illustrates one of the meanings and write a sentence that describes the picture.

Take a Poem Home

Give each child a copy of the poem on page 38 to color or illustrate, practice reading, and then take home to read to a family member. Copies of the students' illustrated poems can also be put into individual poetry scrapbooks that the children can make and decorate.

About the Poet

For more information about Mother Goose, see page 2.

About the Illustrator

Brian Lies was born on February 14, 1963. He does his illustrating in his house in Norfolk, Massachusetts. As a child he loved to invent things, such as two-story doghouses, and then draw diagrams for them. His interest in illustrating came about in the fifth grade when Harry Devlin, an illustrator, visited his school. Lies says that if he weren't an illustrator he would still like to be involved in creating art for children—maybe as an inventor of mechanical toys.

Lies used acrylic paints to create the illustration for "Hey, Diddle, Diddle!" He advises would-be artists to *read* as much as possible, and *look* at lots of art. "If you don't know lots of different stuff, you may be the best artist in the world, but your art will be empty of ideas..."

Hey, Diddle, Diddle!

Hey, diddle, diddle!
The cat and the fiddle.
The cow jumped over the moon.
The little dog laughed
To see such sport,
And the dish ran away with the spoon.

Traditional

One, Two, Three

Day 1

Introduce the Poem

Read the poem "One, Two, Three" to the children. Try to reflect the natural rhythm of the poem as you read it through for the first time. Allow the students to absorb the language and to think about what pictures the poem brings to mind. Discuss the illustration and any unfamiliar concepts or vocabulary such as *right.*

Discuss the Poem

Invite the children to respond to the poem.

- **Can you show me your little right finger?**
- **What do you call the little finger on each hand?**
- **What types of things would you take with you to go fishing?**
- **What would make a fish bite you?**

Day 2

Reread the Poem

Reread the poem "One, Two, Three" with the children, encouraging them to join in when they feel comfortable. Continue to discuss the poem and the illustration.

Discuss the Poem

Encourage the children to think about the poem and the illustration.

- **Have you ever caught a fish? If so, what did you do with it?**
- **Do you think it would hurt if a fish bit you? Why or why not?**
- **Where could the people in the illustration be fishing? How can you tell?**

Focus on Phonological Awareness

Rhyming

Read the poem to the children. On lines two, four, six, and eight, pause before the rhyming words and allow the students to complete each rhyme. Then say the word *ten* and invite the students to brainstorm additional words that rhyme with *ten.*

Play a Matching Game

Paper clip a blank transparency over the poster. Have children orally count the fish in the illustration and then number the fish (1–10) with a marker on the transparency. Then provide cards with the numerals 1–10 and have volunteers match the numeral cards to the number words in the poem.

Day 3

Reread the Poem

Read the poem. Point to the text to stress one-to-one correspondence and directionality. Invite children to move to the rhythm of the poem in some way, such as bouncing, swaying, or rocking. Read the poem again and this time allow the children to play instruments such as rhythm sticks, drums, maracas, bells, and tambourines to the rhythm.

Focus on Phonological Awareness

Syllable Awareness

Read the poem and have children clap once for each syllable they hear. As they hear and clap each syllable, the rhythm of the poem can be enjoyed.

Write an Innovation

Have children write an innovation of the poem by replacing the word *fish* with the name of another animal. Provide children with a copy of the poem that has the word *fish* omitted so that they do not have to rewrite the entire poem. Children can illustrate and share their new poems. You can also have the children "fish" for an animal name. Attach a string to a long stick. Tie a magnet onto the free end of the string. Cut out, laminate, and place magnetic tape on animal pictures. Place the pictures in a large fish bowl. Allow the students to "fish" out animals to use in their poems.

Day 4

Reread the Poem

Read the poem while pointing to the words. Encourage the children to think of hand motions for each line. Reread the poem and invite students to do the hand motions. Then introduce the sequencing images on page 43. Make a photocopy and cut the images apart. Attach each image to an ice-cream stick. Invite the children to retell the poem in their own words using the sequencing images.

Focus on Phonological Awareness

***Phonemic Awareness: Initial Sound* /f/**

Have children listen for words that begin with the */f/* sound. When they hear a word beginning with the */f/* sound, have children wiggle their right pinky finger.

Focus on Phonics

Initial Consonants

Have the children do a word sorting activity with words from the poem. Children can copy words from the poem onto small cards or fish-shaped cutouts. Invite them to sort the words according to the initial sounds. Have the children sort the words into piles or onto large fishbowls cut out of construction paper.

Play "Go Fish"

Make two sets of cards of the number words *one* through *ten* for each pair of children in the class. Invite the children to play "go fish" with the cards.

Day 5

Reread the Poem

Read the poem chorally, pointing to the words as you read. You may want to read the odd-numbered lines and ask the children to read the even-numbered lines. You may also divide the class into two groups and then invite the groups to alternate reading each line.

Focus on Phonological Awareness

Segmenting and Blending

Slowly segment each number word in the poem. Then have students blend the sounds and tell you the word; for example, "If I say */s/ /i/ /ks/*, you would say */s/ /i/ /ks/*, six."

Focus on Phonics

***Word Family* -en**

Write a large numeral 10 on chart paper. Brainstorm words in the *-en* word family. As children suggest a word, write it on the chart.

Take a Poem Home

Give each child a copy of the poem on page 42 to color or illustrate, practice reading, and then take home to read to a family member. Copies of the students' illustrated poems can also be put into individual poetry scrapbooks that the children can make and decorate.

About the Poet

For more information about Mother Goose, see page 2.

About the Illustrator

Daniel T. Powers was born on October 15, 1959. He does most of his illustrating in his studio, which is perched atop the Manzano Mountains in New Mexico. His ideas and inspiration sprout from just about everywhere and everything, including past experiences, his love of beauty, other cultures, and people. For the child interested in becoming an illustrator, he is encouraging. "Keep at it...disregard discouraging words...and love what you're doing." If he weren't an illustrator, Powers says he would love to be a musician—he plays the hammered dulcimer in a folk group. Powers used watercolor paints to create the illustration for "One, Two, Three."

One, Two, Three

One, two, three, four, five,
Once I caught a fish alive.
Six, seven, eight, nine, ten,
But I let it go again.
Why did you let it go?
Because it bit my finger so.
Which finger did it bite?
The little finger on the right.

Traditional

Fuzzy Wuzzy

Day 1

Introduce the Poem

Read the poem "Fuzzy Wuzzy" to the children. Try to reflect the natural rhythm of the poem as you read it through for the first time. Allow the students to absorb the language and to think about what pictures the poem brings to mind. Discuss the illustration and any unfamiliar concepts or vocabulary such as *fuzzy* and the nonsense word *wuzzy*.

Discuss the Poem

Invite the children to respond to the poem.

- **Do you have a favorite teddy bear? If so, what makes it special?**
- **Why do you suppose Fuzzy Wuzzy had no hair?**
- **If Fuzzy Wuzzy had no hair, why was his name Fuzzy Wuzzy?**

Day 2

Reread the Poem

Reread the poem "Fuzzy Wuzzy" with the children, encouraging them to join in when they feel comfortable. Continue to discuss the poem and the illustration.

Discuss the Poem

Encourage the children to think about the poem and the illustration.

- **Can you think of some other things that are fuzzy?**
- **Which would you prefer, a bear with hair or a bear without hair? Why?**
- **What do you notice about the way this poem sounds?**

Focus on Phonological Awareness

Rhyming

Read the poem aloud. Have children listen for the words that rhyme *(Fuzzy/Wuzzy, bear/hair)* and ask them to growl like a bear when they hear them.

Make Your Own Fuzzy Wuzzy

Collect materials with a variety of textures such as corduroy, felt, velvet, wool, cotton, lace, nylon, and fake fur. Cut the fabric into patches similar to those in the poster illustration. Enlarge and photocopy the picture of the bear without hair. Glue the copies onto large sheets of cardstock paper. Invite the children to make their own Fuzzy Wuzzy by gluing fabric patches to their bear. Each bear will be a little different and fun to touch and share.

Day 3

Reread the Poem

Read the poem. Point to the text to stress one-to-one correspondence and directionality. Read the poem again, this time encouraging the children to read it faster to reflect its tongue-twister qualities. Then introduce the bear pictures on page 47. Make a copy for each child. Invite students to color, cut out, and then glue the images back to back on an ice-cream stick. Reread the poem and encourage the children to use the puppets to act out the poem.

Focus on Phonological Awareness

Phonemic Awareness: Manipulating

Substitute the initial sound /*f*/ in *Fuzzy* with other consonant sounds as you read the poem; for example, *Nuzzy Wuzzy* instead of *Fuzzy Wuzzy*. Continue with other sounds that the children suggest.

Make a Graph

Invite each child to bring his or her favorite teddy bear to class. Use the bears to make a graph. Choose categories such as fur, length, color, and size, and graph the different bear characteristics.

Day 4

Reread the Poem

Read the poem while pointing to the words. Encourage the children to snap or clap to the rhythm of the poem. Next, write each line of the poem on a sentence strip. Have the children sequence the poem sentence strips in a pocket chart.

Focus on Phonological Awareness

Alliteration

Read the last line of the poem to the children and ask them to listen for words that begin with the same sound.

- **What sound did you hear repeated?**

Focus on Mechanics

Capitalization

Have the children distinguish between uppercase and lowercase letters in the poem. Write the following letters on self-stick notes: *F, f, W, w.* Have the children match the letters on the notes to the letters in the poem by placing the notes over the letters.

Compare and Contrast with a Venn Diagram

Make a large Venn diagram. Label one circle "Real Bear" and the other circle "Teddy Bear." Brainstorm things the children know about each type of bear and write them on the Venn diagram in the appropriate place. Then invite the children to use the diagram to compare and contrast real bears to teddy bears.

Day 5

Reread the Poem

Read the poem, pointing to the words as you read. You might want to encourage the children to take turns pointing to the words while you reread the poem.

Focus on Phonological Awareness

Phonemic Awareness: Segmenting

Use sound-segment boxes to segment the sounds found in several words from the poem *(fuzzy, no, had, he).* As you slowly articulate each word, move an object such as a button into each box from left to right. Have students segment the words with you. You might want to invite individual students to come up and move the object into each box as the sounds are articulated. Have the children blend each word after they segment it.

Focus on Phonics

Medial Consonant /z/

Have children locate the */z/* sound in *Fuzzy* and *Wuzzy*. Ask them to find another word with the */z/* sound that doesn't have the letter *z*.

Take a Poem Home

Give each child a copy of the poem on page 46 to color or illustrate, practice reading, and then take home to read to a family member. Copies of the students' illustrated poems can also be put into individual poetry scrapbooks that the children can make and decorate.

About the Illustrator

Susan Calitri was born on July 9, 1964. She works out of her studio in North Kingstown, Rhode Island. As a child, Calitri drew all kinds of things, including dogs, cats, and teddy bears. After working full time for ten years for a greeting card company, she decided to work for herself and took a turn at freelance illustrating. She enjoys drawing fun, colorful, and happy things. "[It's] the perfect thing for kids."

To create the illustration for "Fuzzy Wuzzy," Calitri used watercolor and acrylic paints, colored pencils, and fabrics. Her advice to aspiring illustrators is straightforward. "Draw, draw, draw—every day. It's the only thing that really works."

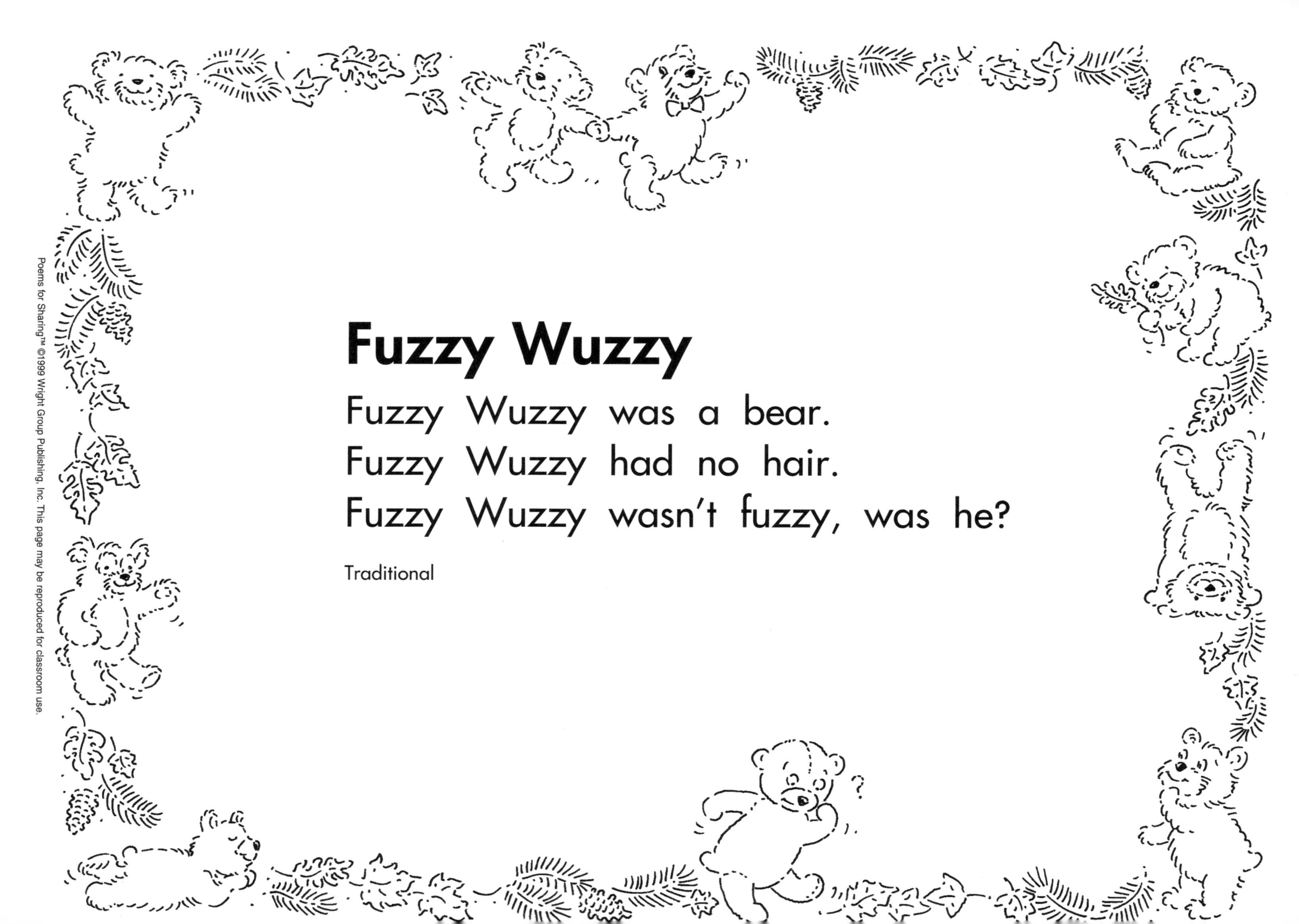

Fuzzy Wuzzy

Fuzzy Wuzzy was a bear.
Fuzzy Wuzzy had no hair.
Fuzzy Wuzzy wasn't fuzzy, was he?

Traditional

Way Down South

Day 1

Introduce the Poem

Read the poem "Way Down South" to the children. Try to reflect the natural rhythm of the poem as you read it through for the first time. Allow the students to absorb the language and to think about what pictures the poem brings to mind. Discuss the illustration and any unfamiliar concepts or vocabulary such as *South* and the phrase "Pick on somebody your own size."

Discuss the Poem

Invite the children to respond to the poem.

- **What does "Pick on somebody your own size" mean? Do you agree with this idea?**
- **Can you show or tell me what *South* is?**
- **Why do you suppose the grasshopper stepped on the elephant's toe?**
- **Do you think it would hurt if a grasshopper stepped on your toe? Why or why not?**

Day 2

Reread the Poem

Reread the poem "Way Down South" with the children, encouraging them to join in when they feel comfortable. Continue to discuss the poem and the illustration.

Discuss the Poem

Encourage the children to think about the poem and the illustration.

- **Does this poem remind you of any experiences that you have had?**
- **How do you think the elephant is feeling? How can you tell?**
- **How could the grasshopper make the elephant feel better?**
- **Can you think of some other animals the size of a grasshopper? An elephant?**

Focus on Phonological Awareness

Rhyming

Read the poem to the children. In lines two and four, read the text up to the rhyming word and then stop. Have the children say the words that would complete the rhymes *(toe* and *size).*

Illustrate a Sentence

Have the children illustrate the sentence "Pick on somebody your own size." Share the illustrations.

Day 3

Reread the Poem

Read the poem. Point to the text to stress one-to-one correspondence and directionality. Invite pairs of children to play the roles of the elephant and the grasshopper and dramatize the poem. You might want to provide props, costumes, or masks. Then read the poem again, one line at a time. This time allow students to create and do hand motions for each line.

Focus on Phonological Awareness

Phonemic Awareness: Initial Sound /s/

Read the text. Encourage the children to listen for words that begin with the /s/ sound. As children hear a word that begins with *s,* have them point south with their thumbs. You may need to show the children which direction south is. Then brainstorm additional words that begin with the /s/ sound.

Learn to Blend Colors

Discuss the illustration. Point out how the colors in the illustration are blended together. Then give each child a sheet of white paper. Provide colored chalk, scissors, and cotton balls. Have the children select a color and scrape the sides of the chalk with the edge of their scissors over their paper. Ask the children to rub the chalk flakes with a cotton ball. Then invite them to choose another color of chalk and scrape it with their scissors. When the children rub the chalk flakes with the cotton ball this time, they will blend the two colors together. Encourage the children to continue with as many colors as they would like. Once children are familiar with this activity, they can draw a picture and color it using this technique.

Day 4

Reread the Poem

Read the poem while pointing to the words. Then have the children read the poem, getting louder for each line and finally shouting the last line.

Focus on Phonological Awareness

Phonemic Awareness: Medial Sound /ō/

Tell the children that you will read the poem, stop at different words, and ask them to decide if the word you stop at has an */ō/* sound. Stop at some words that do and some words that do not.

Focus on Phonics

***Initial Consonant Blend* gr**

Have students frame the words *grow* and *grasshopper* in the poem. Ask them to tell you how they are alike. Together make a list of other words that begin with *gr*.

Locate Places

Brainstorm and discuss places that the children are familiar with that have north, south, east, and west in the names. Locate some of the places on a globe or a map.

Day 5

Reread the Poem

Read the poem, pointing to the words as you read. Invite the children to use instruments such as rhythm sticks, bells, tambourines, and drums to tap the rhythm of the poem. Then introduce the sequencing images on page 51. Make a photocopy and cut the images apart. Attach the images to ice-cream sticks. Have the children match the images to the words in the poem.

Focus on Phonics

***Long Vowel* o**

On small cards, write the words from the poem that have the long *o* sound and words with other *o* sounds. Place the word cards next to a pocket chart. With the children, sort the words into two categories: words with a long *o* sound and words with other *o* sounds. For each card, hold it up in front of the children, say the word, ask the children if they hear the long *o* sound, and then place it in the appropriate category.

Take a Poem Home

Give each child a copy of the poem on page 50 to color or illustrate, practice reading, and then take home to read to a family member. Copies of the students' illustrated poems can also be put into individual poetry scrapbooks that the children can make and decorate.

About the Illustrator

Felipe Dávalos was born on June 16, 1942. He lived in Mexico most of his life and has been in the United States for three years. He currently works out of his studio in Sacramento, California. Early in his career he did illustrations for advertisements. This eventually led to offers to do book illustrations. Once he got into book work, he found he really enjoyed it. Dávalos especially enjoys illustrating for children. He feels his contributions to children's books allow him to give back to kids the joy he received from picture books as a child. Dávalos used acrylic paints to create the illustration for "Way Down South."

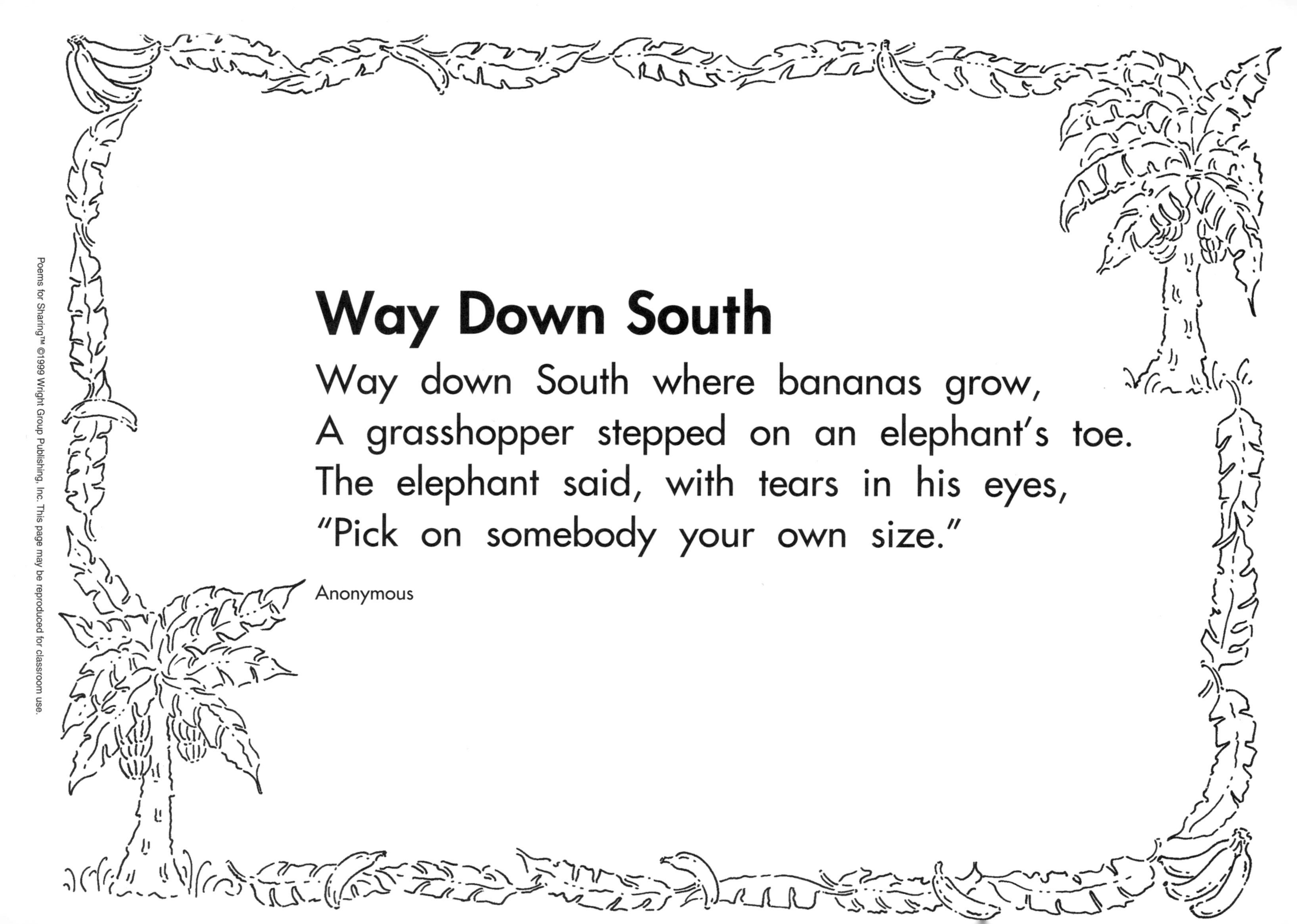

Way Down South

Way down South where bananas grow,
A grasshopper stepped on an elephant's toe.
The elephant said, with tears in his eyes,
"Pick on somebody your own size."

Anonymous

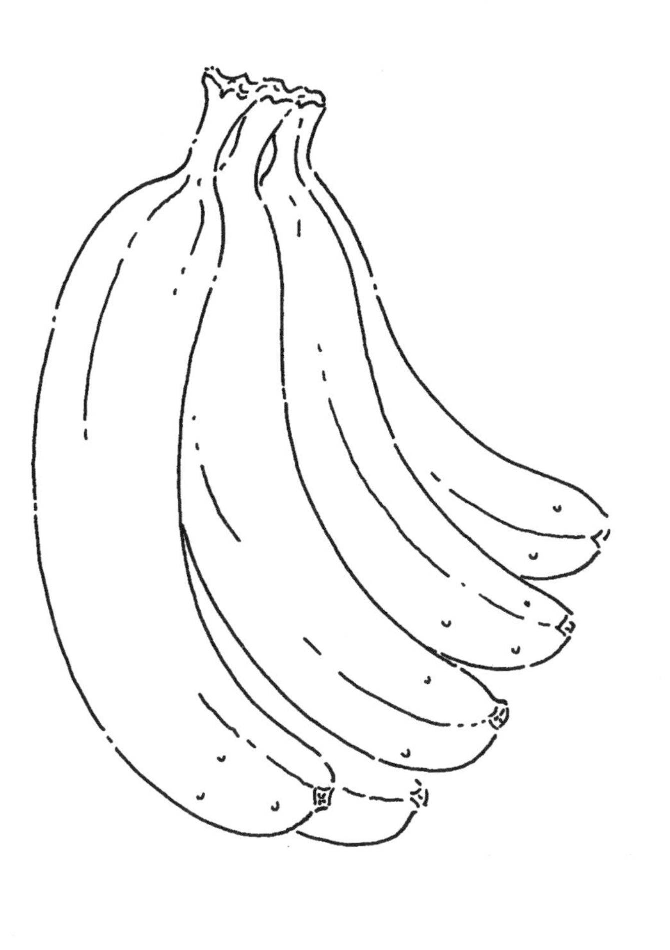

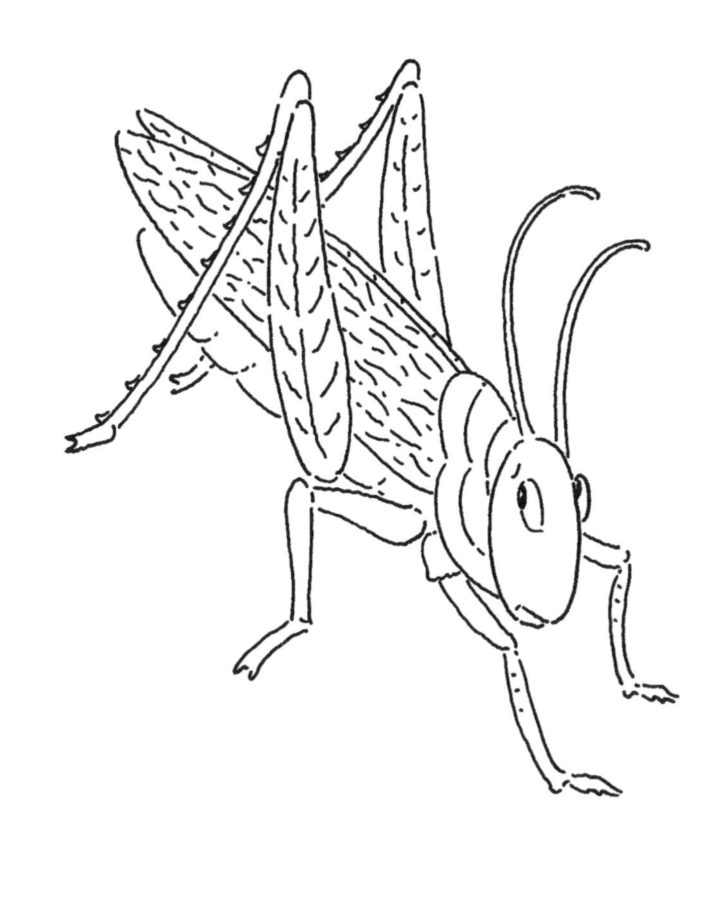

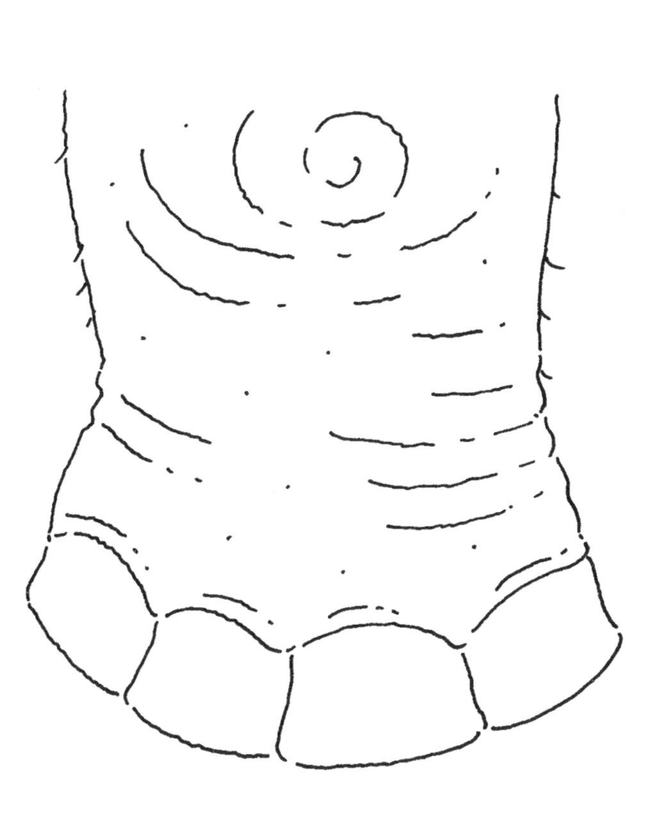

Peter Piper

Day 1

Introduce the Poem

Read the poem "Peter Piper" to the children. Try to reflect the natural rhythm of the poem as you read it through for the first time. Allow the students to absorb the language and to think about what pictures the poem brings to mind. Discuss the illustration and any unfamiliar concepts or vocabulary such as *pickled* and *peck*. A *peck* is a quarter of a *bushel*. Both bushels and pecks are units of dry measurement. You also might want to explain that a peck is equivalent to eight quarts.

Discuss the Poem

Invite the children to respond to the poem.

- **Do you notice anything about the way this poem sounds?**
- **If you were Peter Piper, what would you do with a peck of pickled peppers?**
- **Why do you suppose Peter Piper only picked a peck of peppers instead of a whole bushel?**
- **Can you think of any other fruits or vegetables that you can pick?**

Day 2

Reread the Poem

Reread the poem "Peter Piper" with the children, encouraging them to join in when they feel comfortable. Continue to discuss the poem and the illustration.

Discuss the Poem

Encourage the children to think about the poem and the illustration.

- **Can you think of any other types of peppers you may have heard of or eaten, such as jalapeño peppers or green, yellow, or red bell peppers?**
- **Have you ever eaten anything that was pickled?**

Focus on Phonological Awareness

Phonemic Awareness: Initial Sound /p/

Read the poem. As you read, have the children listen for the initial sound */p/*. When the children hear a word that begins with the */p/* sound, have them put their thumbs up.

Create Alliterative Phrases

Have the children create alliterative phrases using a format similar to the one in the poem. Invite students to think of a verb and a noun that begin with the initial sound in their first names. Children can then use the structure of "Peter Piper" to write their phrases. Examples might include something like "Maria munched on marshmallows" or "Maria mashed some melting marshmallows." Some children may wish to try adding an adjective to describe their objects. Allow children to illustrate their alliterative phrases.

Day 3

Reread the Poem

Read the poem at a faster rate, reflecting the tongue-twister quality of the poem. Point to the text to stress one-to-one correspondence and directionality. Encourage the children to try to reread the poem as fast as they can. Then invite individual children to read it quickly. If you have the time, introduce the sequencing images on page 55. Make a photocopy and cut the images apart. Attach the images to ice-cream sticks. Have the children match each image to the word in the poem.

Focus on Phonological Awareness

Phonemic Awareness: Initial Sound /p/

Invite children to play a game called "Going to the Grocery Store." Have the children sit in a circle on the floor. Tell the children that today you are going to buy things that begin with the */p/* sound. Begin by saying, "I am going to the grocery store to buy pop-corn." Continue around the circle until each child has had a turn. If a child cannot think of a word that begins with the */p/* sound, tell the child that he or she can pass. Always go back to the children who pass because often another child's item will give them ideas.

Make Pepper Prints

Bring in green, yellow, and red bell peppers. Share the peppers with the children. Then cut the peppers in half. Allow the children to make pepper prints by pressing a piece into paint and then pushing it down onto a sheet of white paper to make a design.

Day 4

Reread the Poem

Read the poem while pointing to the words. Divide the children into four groups. Have each group chorally read a line of the poem.

Focus on Phonological Awareness

Phonemic Awareness: Compare/Contrast

Say the words *Peter* and *Piper*. Then have the children say each word and ask them about the sounds.

- **Do *Peter* and *Piper* begin with the same sound? If so, what sound do they begin with?**
- **Do *Peter* and *Piper* end with the same sound? If so, what sound do they end with?**

Continue with other words in the poem, such as *peppers/where's, picked/pickled,* and *peck/Piper.*

Focus on Concepts of Print

Concept of Letter

Invite children to come up and frame with a framing device the last letter in specific words. For additional practice, write the first line of the poem on a sentence strip. Place the sentence strip in a pocket chart. Then write the last letter of each word on a small card. Have the children match the letter cards to the last letter of each word on the sentence strip.

Taste Some Pickled Food

Discuss other foods besides peppers that are pickled, such as pickles, beets, tomatoes, and eggs. Bring in samples for the children to taste. Be aware of any allergies or other food restrictions students might have. Compare and contrast the flavors.

Day 5

Reread the Poem

Read the poem, pointing to the words as you read. Have the children clap or tap to the rhythm of the poem. Introduce instruments such as tambourines, drums, maracas, and rhythm sticks. Allow children to play the instruments as you reread the poem.

Focus on Phonological Awareness

Phonemic Awareness: Segmenting and Blending

Read the first line of the poem. Then orally segment the word *peck (/p/ /e/ /k/)*. Have the children do the same thing and ask them what they hear.

- **What sound do you hear at the beginning of *peck?* At the end? In the middle?**

After you orally segment *peck*, blend the sounds together and say the whole word.

Focus on Vocabulary

Multiple Meaning Word

Discuss the multiple meanings of the word *peck*. Give examples such as the following definitions: a quarter of a bushel, a light kiss, or to poke at something. Have the children select one of the meanings to illus-trate. Then have each child write a sentence about the illustration.

Take a Poem Home

Give each child a copy of the poem on page 54 to color or illustrate, practice reading, and then take home to read to a family member. Copies of the stu-dents' illustrated poems can also be put into individ-ual poetry scrapbooks that the children can make and decorate.

About the Poet

For more information about Mother Goose, see page 2.

Peter Piper

Peter Piper picked a peck of pickled peppers;
A peck of pickled peppers Peter Piper picked.
If Peter Piper picked a peck of pickled peppers,
Where's the peck of pickled peppers Peter Piper picked?

Traditional

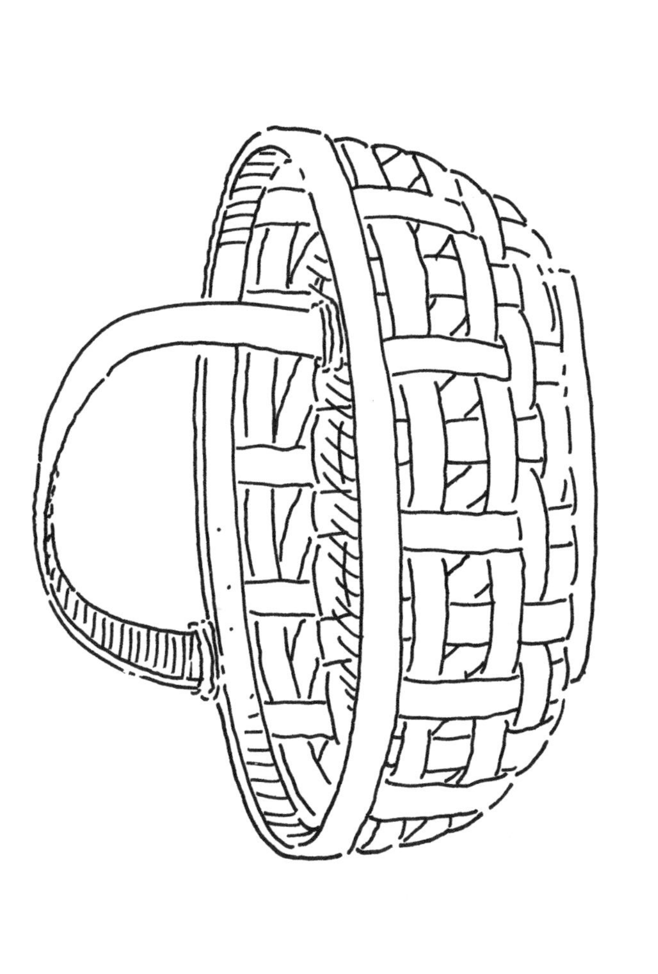

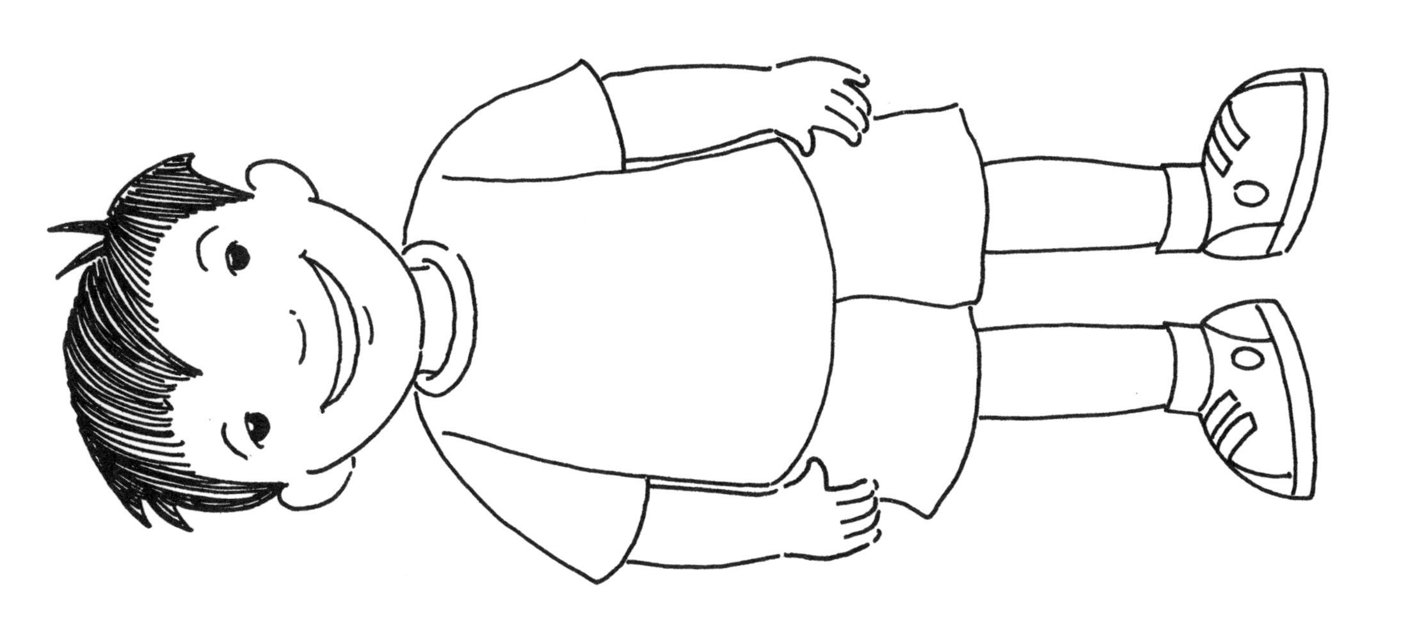

The Thorn Song

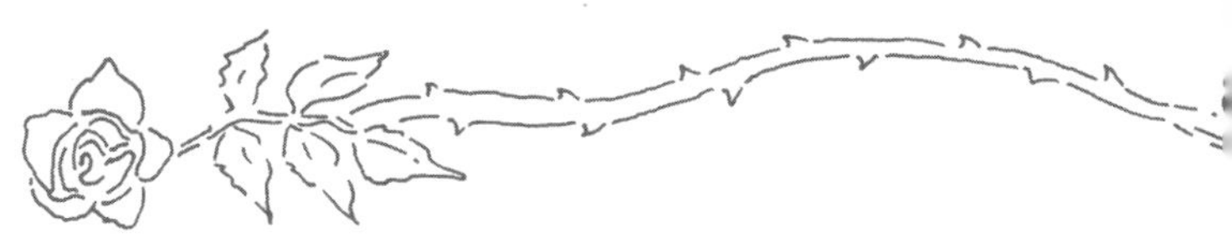

Day 1

Introduce the Poem

Read the poem "The Thorn Song" to the children. Try to reflect the natural rhythm of the poem as you read it through for the first time. Allow the students to absorb the language and to think about what pictures the poem brings to mind. Discuss the illustration and any unfamiliar concepts or vocabulary such as *still, thorn,* and *wild rose.*

Discuss the Poem

Invite the children to respond to the poem.

- **Can you explain the difference between a rose and a wild rose?**
- **What does "held me still" mean?**
- **How do you suppose the girl in the illustration feels?**
- **Have you ever had something like this happen to you before?**

Day 2

Reread the Poem

Reread the poem "The Thorn Song" with the children, encouraging them to join in when they feel comfortable. Continue to discuss the poem and the illustration.

Discuss the Poem

Encourage the children to think about the poem and the illustration.

- **Have you ever felt a thorn? What was it like?**
- **What are some reasons the girl might have for wanting to get home before dark?**
- **Where do you think she is going?**

Focus on Phonological Awareness

Rhyming

Have the children complete the rhymes as you read the poem orally. For example, read the first and second lines of the poem up to the word *still* and then stop. Ask the children to fill in the word that rhymes with *hill (still).* Continue with the third and fourth lines of the poem.

Write a Poem

Bring a real rose to class. Have the children brainstorm words that describe the rose. List them on a piece of chart paper. Have the children use the words to write a poem about roses. You might want to use a simple format such as the following example:

Title: Roses
Roses look pretty.
Roses feel soft.
Roses smell sweet.
I like yellow roses.

Day 3

Reread the Poem

Read the poem. Point to the text to stress one-to-one correspondence and directionality. Then encourage students to dramatize the poem while you reread it. Next, introduce the sequencing images on page 59 for "The Thorn Song." Make photocopies and give each child a copy. Have the children cut out the sequencing images and attach them to ice-cream sticks. Allow the children to dramatize the poem using the images.

Focus on Phonological Awareness

Phonemic Awareness: Manipulating

Have the children subtract sounds from the words *hill* and *still* to make a new word *(ill).* First, slowly articulate the word *hill.* Have children do the same. Ask the children what would be left if the */h/* sound were taken away from *hill.* Then slowly articulate the word *still.* Ask students what would be left if the */st/* sound were taken away from *still.*

Make a Mural

Make a mural of a large, wild rosebush similar to the one in the illustration. Label the mural, "'You thorns,' I said..." Then invite the children to draw pictures of themselves. Staple the pictures to the mural and give each child a speech bubble. Have the children respond to the sentence on the mural by writing what they would say to the rosebush; for example, "Don't poke me!" or "Let me go!"

Day 4

Reread the Poem

Read the poem while pointing to the words. You may wish to have individual children pantomime a line while the rest of the children try to guess the action.

Focus on Phonological Awareness

Phonemic Awareness: Compare/Contrast

Have the children compare words by their beginning sound. Read the following words from the poem: *hill, held, dark, hold.* Ask children to tell you which word begins with a different sound. Continue with *was, must, walking,* and *wild.*

Focus on Word Structure

Contractions

Point out the contractions *don't* and *it's* in the poem. Explain what a contraction is and that these are examples of contractions. Then write lines three and four of the poem on sentence strips. Place them in a pocket chart. Write *do not* and *it is* on small cards. Have the children match these cards to the contractions in the text. Discuss what makes the poem sound better—the contractions or the complete words?

Make a Flower Picture

Have each child draw a colorful flower. Then encourage children to write descriptions of their flowers.

Day 5

Reread the Poem

Make a transparency of the blackline master of the poem on page 58. Place the poem on the overhead projector and read it, pointing to the words as you read. Allow individual students to take turns pointing to the words on the screen or wall with a pointer as the poem is reread. A fake rose stem makes a fun pointer for this activity.

Focus on Phonological Awareness

Onset and Rime

Say the word *rose* to the children. Orally segment the onset */r/* from the sound that the rime *-ose* makes. Then have children do the same thing. Ask students to think of other words that can be made with the same *-ose* rime, such as *hose, nose, pose,* and *chose.*

Focus on Vocabulary

Content and High Frequency Words

Play "What Word Can You Show Us?" with the children. Invite individual children to come up and show the rest of the children a word they know in the poem. Invite the students to locate and frame the word and then read it to the class.

Take a Poem Home

Give each child a copy of the poem on page 58 to color or illustrate, practice reading, and then take home to read to a family member. Copies of the students' illustrated poems can also be put into individual poetry scrapbooks that the children can make and decorate.

About the Illustrator

Yoriko Ito was born on April 9, 1967. She works out of her studio in Hollywood, California. As a child, Ito always enjoyed drawing and painting. Luckily she was able to make a career out of something she loves to do. She enjoys illustrating stories, especially children's stories. Ito created the illustration for "The Thorn Song" by using *gouache (GWOSH),* acrylic paints, and ink. Gouache is a method of painting in which white is added to watercolor paint for an opaque effect. Her advice to aspiring illustrators? "Spend lots of time drawing...stay true to your dreams...and listen to your heart."

The Thorn Song

I was walking there along the hill
When a wild rose caught and held me still.
"You thorns," I said, "don't hold me so:
It's getting dark and I must go."

Traditional Japanese rhyme

Six Little Ducks

Day 1

Introduce the Poem

Read the poem "Six Little Ducks" to the children. Try to reflect natural rhythm of the poem as you read it through for the first time. Allow the students to absorb the language and to think about what pictures the poem brings to mind. Discuss the illustration and any unfamiliar concepts or vocabulary such as *fair*.

Discuss the Poem

Invite the children to respond to the poem.

- **What pictures does this poem bring to mind?**
- **Have you ever seen ducks like these? If so, where?**
- **How are these ducks alike and different?**
- **Why do you think the duck with the feather on his back is the leader?**

Day 2

Reread the Poem

Reread the poem "Six Little Ducks" with the children, encouraging them to join in when they feel comfortable. Continue to discuss the poem and the illustration.

Discuss the Poem

Encourage the children to think about the poem and the illustration.

- **What words did you hear that rhymed?**
- **Where do you suppose these ducks are going?**
- **How do these ducks feel? How can you tell?**

Focus on Phonological Awareness

Phonemic Awareness: Initial Sound /f/

Read the first four lines of the poem. Ask children to listen for the words that begin with the */f/* sound. Brainstorm other words they know that begin with */f/*.

Brainstorm and Write an Innovation

Brainstorm a list of animals, the sound that each animal makes, and things the animals could have on their backs. Write ideas on a piece of chart paper. The following is an example:

animal	sound	object on back
cow	moo	grass
dog	woof	bone
cat	meow	stripe

Use the chart to write an innovation of the poem. Place self-stick notes over each of the following words in the poem: *ducks, duck, feather, quack*. Ask the children to pick new words from the chart to replace these. Write their words on the self-stick notes. Then read the new poem together.

Day 3

Reread the Poem

Read the poem, pointing to the text as you read. Invite students to quack like a duck when they come to the word *quack*. Reread the poem again and encourage the students to quack and flap their arms like a duck flaps its wings when they read the word *quack*.

Focus on Phonological Awareness

Onset and Rime

Say the word *back* from the poem. Model changing *back* to *quack* by taking off the initial sound */b/*.

- **If I take off /b/ and add /kw/, what new word do we have?**

Continue with other onsets such as */p/*, */r/*, */s/*, and */t/*.

Write a Story

Have students write stories about themselves and what they would do with a feather. Invite each child to illustrate the story.

Day 4

Reread the Poem

Read the poem while pointing to the words. Encourage children to create hand motions for each line of the poem. Then introduce the blackline picture of the leader duck at the top and the five other ducks underneath, found on page 63 of this booklet. Make photocopies and give each child a copy. Model how they can make the ducks appear and disappear by folding the paper in half. Allow children to practice. Reread the poem and invite the children to fold and unfold the picture when they hear the line, "He led the others with a quack, quack, quack!"

Focus on Phonological Awareness

Phonemic Awareness: Segmenting and Blending

Have the children blend phonemes to make words from the poem.

- **What word would you have if you put the sounds /s/ /i/ /ks/ together?**

Continue with other words such as *duck, led, fat,* and *quack.*

Focus on Phonics

Initial Consonant q

Have the children locate all the *qu* words in the poem. Discuss the sound that *qu* makes. Brainstorm other *qu* words and write them on a piece of chart paper. Place the chart paper in a location where the children can add to the list as they encounter additional words that begin with *qu.*

Describe a Duck

Have children locate descriptive words in the poem such as *little, fat, skinny,* and *fair.* Encourage them to point to each word or use some sort of framing device. List the children's words on a piece of chart paper. Then have each child select a descriptive word and draw or paint a picture of a duck that fits that description. Encourage students to label the illustrations.

Day 5

Reread the Poem

Read the poem, pointing to the words as you read. Select six children to pretend to be ducks. Have the children stand in a line. Give the leader duck a feather to hold against his or her back. Ask the child to waddle around the room and encourage the other children to follow. Invite the rest of the children to recite the poem. Continue until all of the children have had a turn. You might also like to invite the children to sing the poem.

Focus on Phonological Awareness

Word Awareness

Give each child a real or paper feather. Tell the children to listen for the word *quack* in the poem. Each time they hear the word *quack,* have them stick the feather in their hair.

Focus on Mechanics

Punctuation: Comma

Discuss the use of commas to separate items in a series. Read line two of the poem as an example. Invite the children to find other examples in the text (lines 4–7).

Take a Poem Home

Give each child a copy of the poem on page 62 to color or illustrate, practice reading, and then take home to read to a family member. Copies of the students' illustrated poems can also be put into individual poetry scrapbooks that the children can make and decorate.

About the Illustrator

Diana Magnuson was born on February 17, 1947. She works out of her home in Marquette, Michigan. Magnuson enjoys illustrating for children because it makes her feel good knowing that her work is doing something positive for them. Ideas for her illustrations come from the manuscript and art suggestions from the publisher, and then she uses her imagination and reference materials collected over the years. Magnuson used watercolor paints and ink to create the illustration for "Six Little Ducks." For the child who wants to become an illustrator, she has this advice: "Love it. Draw what YOU enjoy drawing. Draw the things that bring you joy..."

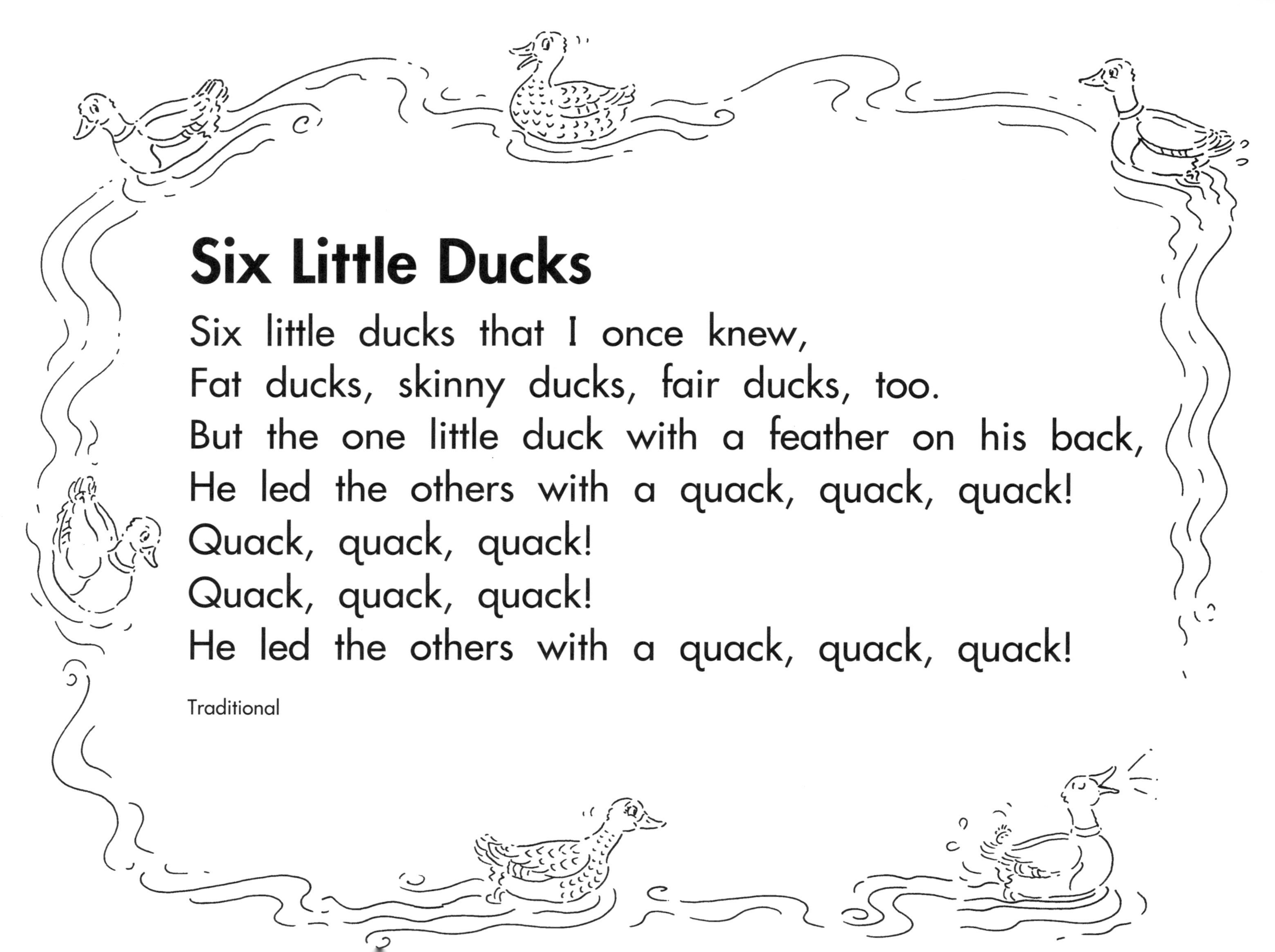

Six Little Ducks

Six little ducks that I once knew,
Fat ducks, skinny ducks, fair ducks, too.
But the one little duck with a feather on his back,
He led the others with a quack, quack, quack!
Quack, quack, quack!
Quack, quack, quack!
He led the others with a quack, quack, quack!

Traditional

Little Bo-Peep

Day 1

Introduce the Poem

Read the poem "Little Bo-Peep" to the children. Try to reflect the natural rhythm of the poem as you read it through for the first time. Allow the students to absorb the language and to think about what pictures the poem brings to mind. Discuss the illustration and any unfamiliar concepts or vocabulary such as *wagging*.

Discuss the Poem

Invite the children to respond to the poem.

- **Have you ever lost anything? If so, how did it make you feel?**
- **What do you suppose Little Bo-Peep is thinking?**
- **What is meant by "wagging their tails"?**
- **If you were Little Bo-Peep, where would you look for your lost sheep?**

Day 2

Reread the Poem

Reread the poem "Little Bo-Peep" with the children, encouraging them to join in when they feel comfortable. Discuss the rhymes found within the lines of the poem.

Discuss the Poem

Encourage the children to think about the poem and the illustration.

- **Can you think of some ways Little Bo-Peep could prevent her sheep from getting lost again?**
- **How do you keep your pets from getting lost?**
- **Why do you think the sheep will come home if she leaves them alone?**

Focus on Phonological Awareness

Rhyming

Read the first line of the poem. Have the children listen for the rhyming words *Peep* and *sheep*. Then play a game with the children using additional words that rhyme with *Peep* and *sheep*. Begin by saying, "I am thinking of a word that rhymes with *Peep* and *sheep*. It means to..." The children have to determine the word; for example, "I am thinking of a word that rhymes with *Peep* and *sheep*. It is the sound a horn makes." The children would respond, "Beep!" Continue with other rhyming words.

Make a Mural

Create a wall mural. Have each child paint or draw a picture of a sheep. Select one child to paint or draw Little Bo-Peep. Create the background for the mural with large sheets of colored butcher paper. (Refer to the illustration for ideas.) Attach the sheep and Little Bo-Peep to the mural background. Write the poem and place it on the mural. Encourage children to read the familiar poem on the wall during center time.

Day 3

Reread the Poem

Read the poem. Point to the text to stress one-to-one correspondence and directionality. Encourage children to think of actions or hand motions for each line. Reread the poem again, this time including the actions or hand motions. Introduce the sequencing images on page 67. Make photocopies and give each child a copy. Allow children to make stick puppets using the images and ice-cream sticks. Have children dramatize the poem using the stick puppets.

You can also create puppets for the overhead projector center. Make transparencies of the sequencing images and place them at the center with a transparency of the poem. Invite children to illustrate the poem transparency and then use the sequencing images with the poem to dramatize it.

Focus on Phonological Awareness

Syllable Awareness

Have children listen for and clap the syllables they hear in each word that you read in the poem.

Create a Feature Analysis Chart

Have children complete a feature analysis chart of different animals and the types of tails they have. Here is an example of the chart:

	fat	long	thin	straight	short
sheep					X
dog	X	X	X	X	X
cat	X	X	X	X	X
pig					X
horse		X	X		

Include other features such as curly and fuzzy. When the chart is completed, have children summarize the results.

Day 4

Reread the Poem

Read the poem while pointing to the words. You may wish to personalize the poem by substituting the name of a child in the class for Little Bo-Peep. Continue rereading the poem, substituting as many names as time allows.

Focus on Phonological Awareness

Phonemic Awareness: Initial Sound /l/

Read the first line of the poem and have students listen for words beginning with the /l/ sound *(little, lost).* Then say pairs of words—one beginning with /l/ and one with another sound. Have children baa like a sheep when they hear an /l/ word.

Focus on Phonics

***Word Family* -eep**

Have students frame the *-eep* word family in *Peep* and *sheep*. Use magnetic letters or letter cards to add onsets to the *-eep* rime.

Create Lost-and-Found Posters

Have the children make lost-and-found posters for Little Bo-Peep to help her find her lost sheep. Encourage children to include pictures and refer to the poem to find words they can use in their posters.

Day 5

Reread the Poem

Select a child to play the part of Little Bo-Peep and several other children to be sheep. As you reread the poem with the rest of the children, ask the actors to dramatize the poem. Continue rereading the poem, selecting a new Little Bo-Peep and sheep each time.

Focus on Phonological Awareness

Phonemic Awareness: Manipulating

Read line two of the poem, which contains the word *can't.* Slowly articulate each sound. Have the children listen to the sounds. Ask, "What word would be left if the /k/ sound were taken away from *can't?* What word would be left if the /t/ sound were taken away from *can't?"*

Focus on Phonics

***Initial Consonant* l**

Ask the students to brainstorm nouns and adjectives that begin with the letter *l* and write them down. Then provide the following writing structure for the children to complete with words from the *l* word list: Little Bo-Peep has lost her ______.

Take a Poem Home

Give each child a copy of the poem on page 66 to color or illustrate, practice reading, and then take home to read to a family member. Copies of the students' illustrated poems can also be put into individual poetry scrapbooks that the children can make and decorate.

About the Poet

For more information about Mother Goose, see page 2.

About the Illustrator

R. W. Alley was born on December 30, 1955. Inspiration for his ideas come from his interest in everything around him. Alley likes illustrating for children because children's books have the most interesting stories, and, he says, "Children care about pictures." If he weren't illustrating, he would like to try his hand at writing stories.

Alley used a pen-and-ink and watercolor paint technique to create the illustration for "Little Bo-Peep." He advises children who are interested in becoming illustrators to "read...keep a sketch pad...[and] draw every day."

Little Bo-Peep

Little Bo-Peep has lost her sheep
And can't tell where to find them.
Leave them alone and they'll come home,
Wagging their tails behind them.

From the traditional rhyme

Wright Group Book Links

Blast Off!

The Story Box®
Dan, the Flying Man (Read-Togethers 2)
**The Jigaree* (Read-Togethers 1)

SUNSHINE™
"Little Puppy" Rap (Read-Togethers, Set 3)
Ten Happy Elephants (Read-Togethers, Set 3)

TWiG® Books
The Nine Days of Camping (Read-Togethers, Set 1)
Ten Yellow Buses (Read-Togethers, Set 2)

The Story Basket®
Ballyhoo! (Set B)

The Bus Song

The Story Box®
**To Town* (Read-Togethers 1)

TWiG® Books
City Storm (Read-Togethers, Set 1)
Ten Yellow Buses (Read-Togethers, Set 2)

Covers

The Story Box®
Gloves (Read-Togethers 4)
Hairy Bear (Read-Togethers 2)
Lazy Mary (Read-Togethers 3)
One Cold, Wet Night (Read-Togethers 3)
**Sing a Song* (Read-Togethers 1)

SUNSHINE™
Who Loves Getting Wet? (Read-Togethers, Set 3)

The Story Basket®
Time for Bed, Little Bear (Set C)

Fiddle-i-fee

The Story Box®
**Yes, Ma'am* (Read-Togethers 1)

SUNSHINE™
Duck and Hen (Read-Togethers, Set 1)
The Humongous Cat (Read-Togethers, Set 1)
Old Malolo Had a Farm (Read-Togethers, Set 2)
Open Your Mouth! (Read-Togethers, Set 2)

TWiG® Books
In the Chicken Coop (Read-Togethers, Set 1)

Fuzzy Wuzzy

The Story Box®
**Hairy Bear* (Read-Togethers 2)

The Story Basket®
Time for Bed, Little Bear (Set C)

Hey, Diddle, Diddle!

The Story Box®
**Dan, the Flying Man* (Read-Togethers 2)
The Jigaree (Read-Togethers 1)

Just Like Me

The Story Box®
**In a Dark, Dark Wood* (Read-Togethers 1)
The Jigaree (Read-Togethers 1)
What Is in the Closet? (Read-Togethers 4)

SUNSHINE™
Duck and Hen (Read-Togethers, Set 1)
Mrs. Muddle Mud-Puddle (Read-Togethers, Set 2)

TWiG® Books
In the Chicken Coop (Read-Togethers, Set 1)
Some Things Go Together (Read-Togethers, Set 2)

The Story Basket®
Do Not Open This Book! (Set C)
One Stormy Night (Set A)
What Next? (Set A)

Little Bo-Peep

The Story Box®
**Who Will Be My Mother?* (Read-Togethers 2)

TWiG® Books
In the Chicken Coop (Read-Togethers, Set 1)

The Story Basket®
Time for Bed, Little Bear (Set C)

*The poem is featured in the lesson plan for this title in *The Story Box® Early Emergent Teacher Guide.*

Little Boy Blue

The Story Box®
Boo-Hoo (Read-Togethers 3)
**The Farm Concert* (Read-Togethers 1)
Hairy Bear (Read-Togethers 2)
Lazy Mary (Read-Togethers 3)
Mrs. Wishy-Washy (Read-Togethers 1)
Yes, Ma'am (Read-Togethers 1)

SUNSHINE™
Old Malolo Had a Farm (Read-Togethers, Set 2)

TWiG® Books
In the Chicken Coop (Read-Togethers, Set 1)

The Story Basket®
Move Over! (Set C)

The Monsters' Garden Party

The Story Box®
**The Monsters' Party* (Read-Togethers 1)

SUNSHINE™
Cat's Party (Read-Togethers, Set 1)
The Little Yellow Chicken (Read-Togethers, Set 2)
Ten Happy Elephants (Read-Togethers, Set 3)

TWiG® Books
The Nine Days of Camping (Read-Togethers, Set 1)
Ten Yellow Buses (Read-Togethers, Set 2)

The Story Basket®
The Hungry Giant's Birthday Cake (Set C)

Mud

The Story Box®
Meanies (Read-Togethers 2)
**Mrs. Wishy-Washy* (Read-Togethers 1)
The Red Rose (Read-Togethers 2)

SUNSHINE™
The Dippy Dinner Drippers (Read-Togethers, Set 1)

The Story Basket®
Dishy-Washy (Set C)
The Meanies Came to School (Set B)
Splishy-Sploshy (Set C)
Wishy-Washy Day (Set A)

One, Two, Three

The Story Box®
**Grandpa, Grandpa* (Read-Togethers 2)

SUNSHINE™
The Humongous Cat (Read-Togethers, Set 1)
"Little Puppy" Rap (Read-Togethers, Set 3)
Ten Happy Elephants (Read-Togethers, Set 3)

TWiG® Books
Night Diving (Read-Togethers, Set 2)
The Nine Days of Camping (Read-Togethers, Set 1)

Peter Piper

The Story Box®
**Poor Old Polly* (Read-Togethers 2)

SUNSHINE™
Old Malolo Had a Farm (Read-Togethers, Set 2)

The Story Basket®
Goggly Gookers (Set A)

Six Little Ducks

The Story Box®
**Sing a Song* (Read-Togethers 1)
Three Little Ducks (Read-Togethers 2)

SUNSHINE™
Duck and Hen (Read-Togethers, Set 1)

TWiG® Books
In the Chicken Coop (Read-Togethers, Set 1)

The Thorn Song

The Story Box®
**The Red Rose* (Read-Togethers 2)

SUNSHINE™
The Morning Queen (Read-Togethers, Set 2)

Way Down South

The Story Box®
**Meanies* (Read-Togethers 2)

SUNSHINE™
Cat's Party (Read-Togethers, Set 1)
Ten Happy Elephants (Read-Togethers, Set 3)
The Wicked Pirates (Read-Togethers, Set 2)

The Story Basket®
Ballyhoo! (Set B)
Dishy-Washy (Set C)
Greedy Cat's Breakfast (Set B)
The Hungry Giant's Soup (Set A)

The poem is featured in the lesson plan for this title in *The Story Box® Early Emergent Teacher Guide.

Recommended Poetry Books

Bennett, Jill, comp. *Spooky Poems.* New York: Little, Brown and Company, 1989.

Bryan, Ashley, comp. *All Night, All Day: A Child's First Book of African-American Spirituals.* New York: Macmillan Publishing Company, 1991.

Child's First Book of Poems, A. New York: Golden Press, 1981.

Cohn, Amy L., comp. *From Sea to Shining Sea: A Treasury of American Folklore and Folk Songs.* New York: Scholastic Inc., 1993.

dePaola, Tomie, comp. *Tomie dePaola's Book of Poems.* New York: G. P. Putnam's Sons, 1988.

dePaola, Tomie, comp. *Tomie dePaola's Mother Goose.* New York: G. P. Putnam's Sons, 1985.

Florian, Douglas. *Bing Bang Boing.* Orlando, Fla.: Harcourt Brace & Company, 1994.

Giovanni, Nikki. *Vacation Time: Poems for Children.* New York: William Morrow and Company, Inc., 1980.

Graham, Terry Lynne. *Fingerplays and Rhymes: For Always and Sometimes.* Atlanta, Ga.: Humanics Limited, 1984.

Hart, Jane, comp. *Singing Bee! A Collection of Favorite Children's Songs.* New York: Lothrop, Lee & Shepard Books, 1989.

Holley, Cynthia. *Warming Up to Big Books.* Bothell, Wash.: Wright Group Publishing, Inc., 1995.

Hopkins, Lee Bennett, comp. *Questions.* New York: HarperCollins, 1992.

———. *Side by Side: Poems to Read Together.* New York: Simon & Schuster Inc., 1988.

———. *Surprises.* New York: Harper & Row, 1984.

Hudson, Wade and Cheryl Hudson, comps. *How Sweet the Sound: African-American Songs for Children.* New York: Scholastic Inc., 1995.

Kennedy, X. J. and Dorothy M. Kennedy, comps. *Talking Like the Rain: A First Book of Poems.* New York: Little, Brown and Company, 1992.

Lee, Dennis. *Jelly Belly.* Toronto: Macmillan of Canada, 1983.

Livingston, Myra Cohn, comp. *Dilly Dilly Piccalilli.* New York: Macmillan Publishing Company, 1989.

Merriam, Eve. *You Be Good and I'll Be Night: Jump-on-the-Bed Poems.* New York: Morrow Junior Books, 1988.

Moore, Lilian, comp. *Sunflakes: Poems for Children.* New York: Clarion Books, 1992.

Oram, Hiawyn. *Out of the Blue: Poems About Color.* New York: Hyperion Books for Children, 1993.

Pomerantz, Charlotte. *Halfway to Your House.* New York: Greenwillow Books, 1993.

Prelutsky, Jack, comp. *A. Nonny Mouse Writes Again!* New York: Alfred A. Knopf, Inc., 1993.

———. *The Random House Book of Poetry for Children.* New York: Random House, 1983.

———. *Read-Aloud Rhymes for the Very Young.* New York: Alfred A. Knopf, Inc., 1986.

Ra, Carol F., comp. *Trot, Trot to Boston: Play Rhymes for Baby.* New York: Lothrop, Lee & Shepard Books, 1987.

Real Mother Goose, The. 1916. Reprint, New York: Scholastic Inc., 1994.

Schenk de Regniers, Beatrice, Eva Moore, Mary Michaels White, and Jan Carr, comps. *Sing a Song of Popcorn: Every Child's Book of Poems.* New York: Scholastic Inc., 1988.

Slier, Deborah, ed. *Make a Joyful Sound: Poems for Children by African-American Poets.* New York: Scholastic Inc., 1991.

Stevenson, Robert Louis. *A Child's Garden of Verses.* 1885. Reprint, New York: Simon & Schuster Inc., 1981.

Swann, Brian. *Song of the Sky: Versions of Native American Song-Poems.* Amherst, Mass.: The University of Massachusetts Press, 1993.

Whipple, Laura, ed. *Eric Carle's Animals, Animals.* New York: Scholastic Inc., 1989.

Worth, Valerie. *All the Small Poems and Fourteen More.* New York: Farrar, Straus and Giroux, 1994.

Zolotow, Charlotte, comp. *Everything Glistens and Everything Sings.* Orlando, Fla.: Harcourt Brace Jovanovich, 1987.